CW00429985

For Successful Programme Management:
Think MSP™

London: TSO

information & publishing solutions

Published by TSO (The Stationery Office) and available from:

Online
www.tsoshop.co.uk

Mail, Telephone, Fax & E-mail
TSO
PO Box 29, Norwich, NR3 1GN
Telephone orders/General enquiries: 0870 600 5522
Fax orders: 0870 600 5533
E-mail: customer.services@tso.co.uk
Textphone 0870 240 3701

TSO Shops
16 Arthur Street, Belfast BT1 4GD
028 9023 8451 Fax 028 9023 5401
71 Lothian Road, Edinburgh EH3 9AZ
0870 606 5566 Fax 0870 606 5588

TSO@Blackwell and other Accredited Agents

Published for the Office of Government Commerce under licence from the Controller of Her Majesty's Stationery Office.

First published 2007

Second impression 2008

ISBN 9780113310630

N5778974   c10   04/08

Contents

Foreword

Over the years, we have come to know and (almost!) love the term 'project management'. It features in many job descriptions for positions in management and is widely recognized and understood. But increasingly, organizations are realizing that good project management alone will not deliver large-scale changes. To view a large-scale change as 'just one big project' will almost inevitably lead to failure.

In reality, you probably have a series of projects that may be interlinked, sharing resources and are often dependent on the outcome of related activities. In other words, a programme. Once this has been acknowledged you are then able to apply suitable techniques and processes that will help you to deliver your programme, on time and on budget.

The Office of Government Commerce's guidance on programme management has brought together some of the most successful practices for managing large-scale change.

This publication summarizes the key elements of the guidance to provide readers with an understanding of how the methodology works and the benefits that can be expected. This book is a great introduction for anyone looking to develop their knowledge before moving on to the full training scheme.

S. Collier

S Collier

Executive Director
Office of Government Commerce

Acknowledgements

The Office of Government Commerce (OGC) is grateful to Melanie Franklin (Maven Training Ltd) for her significant contribution under contract to the design and development work in writing the content of this publication.

The OGC would also like to thank the following individuals and their organizations for their contributions in reviewing this publication.

REVIEWERS

John Bartlett	Great Stave
John Brinkworth	Serco Group
Bina Champaneria	4Sight Training Ltd
Keith Coleman	BPUG
Neil Coutts	KPMG
Terry Dailey	Deliverables Management Consultants
Charles Fox	Core IS
Geof Leigh	Goaldart Ltd
Simon Marling	United Kingdom Debt Management Office
Hosam Mostafa	Olympic Programme Support Unit
Ruth Murray-Webster	Lucidus Consulting
David Partington	Cranfield School of Management
Trevor Pearson	BPUG
Andrew Richards	Holos Consulting
Magnus Schoeman	Xansa
Edna Stewart	BPUG
Graham Tanfield	Department for Children, Schools and Families
Andy Taylor	APM Group
Peter van der Els	SoZaWe Rotterdam
Sue Vowler	Project Angels
Peter Weaver	The PSO

The OGC would also like to express its gratitude to the Best Practice User Group (BPUG) for coordinating part of the review and to the APM Group for organizing the quality assurance.

Introduction

1   Introduction

Programme management is the coordinated organization, direction and implementation of a dossier of projects and transformation activities to achieve outcomes and realize benefits of strategic importance to a business.

The need for programme management is growing as organizations realize that they cannot achieve large-scale change through the implementation of individual projects and ad hoc activities. Whilst projects and activities deliver outputs including new products, new services and new business processes, benefits from these outputs cannot be realized without coordinated effort across the organization. Without coordination, organizations find that projects are duplicated, sometimes many times over as different departments carry out their own initiatives. There are also problems with contradictory work streams, where one initiative is in direct competition or contravention of another.

Programme management provides coordination and a common direction across the projects, and emphasizes the need for the delivery of benefits as a result of the projects. Whilst the need for management coordination of large-scale effort is not new, the scale of project work now being undertaken within organizations has driven the need for a well thought out, common approach to these problems.

Managing Successful Programmes (MSP) defines a comprehensive set of steps for providing this coordination and direction. The information is contained in a series of processes called the Transformational Flow. It is supported by a number of principles of good management that must be applied to the programme to achieve success.

THE AUDIENCE FOR THIS BOOK

This book introduces the key concepts and techniques of MSP, which represents proven programme management good practice in successfully delivering transformational change across a wide range of public and private sector organizations.

The intended audience is not restricted solely to those already performing a specific programme management role. The concepts and practical explanations are intended as a basic grounding in programme management and specifically MSP. Therefore, anyone who is impacted by programmes or anyone who wishes to find out more about programmes and how they are managed will find this book of benefit. Many project teams now find themselves working within a programme environment, and this book is also relevant to them. The structure of MSP complements best practice in project management, and many of the terms used will be familiar to those already working within a project environment.

THE STRUCTURE OF THIS BOOK

This book is a companion to *Managing Successful Programmes* and is intended as a shorter guide to the subject. The programme management terms, concepts and explanations are the same in both books.

Chapter 1 looks at how programme management fits into the wider context of the organization as a whole and the benefits that can be gained from implementing this approach to programme management. It also examines the barriers to good programme management and suggests how these barriers adversely affect the successful delivery of a programme.

Chapter 2 explains governance, which is the control framework through which programmes deliver their change objectives and remain within corporate visibility and control. The chapter looks at each of the Governance Themes that form the basis of MSP:

■ Organization
■ Vision
■ Leadership and Stakeholder Engagement
■ Benefits Realization Management
■ Blueprint Design and Delivery
■ Planning and Control
■ Business Case
■ Risk Management and Issue Resolution
■ Quality Management

Chapter 3 takes the reader through the Transformational Flow of a programme, which shows the life of a programme from start to finish, and the iterations through which the programme passes as it delivers its outcomes. The six processes of the Transformational Flow of the programme are:

1   Identifying a Programme
2   Defining a Programme
3   Managing the Tranches
4   Delivering the Capability
5   Realizing the Benefits
6   Closing a Programme

For each of these six steps, the following questions are posed and answered to provide greater understanding of the purpose and the benefits of MSP at each point in the life of a programme:

■ What is the purpose of this?
■ What are the benefits?
■ Do I have to do this?
■ What happens if I don't do this?

- How do I get to the next step in the process?
- What questions should I ask to get to the next step?
- Who is involved?
- Are there any examples to help me?

Throughout the book real-life examples of the use of MSP in a variety of programme situations are given to demonstrate how it has been applied in practice.

The appendices contain descriptions of some of the key documentation required to manage a programme using MSP and checklists and suggested agendas to provide practical help in running a programme. There are also details of where to find more information on MSP and the available training and accreditations in this subject.

WHY MSP? THE STRATEGIC CONTEXT

Programme management principles provide structure and processes to support all types of change. However, it is important to remember that using programme management requires significant resourcing, including the provision of appropriately skilled and experienced individuals, which requires relatively high levels of funding. Therefore, programme management is best applied to change that has high levels of complexity, ambiguity and risk.

MSP is best used in situations of transformational change rather than incremental change. Transformational change concentrates on transforming the way business functions, putting in place new structures, systems, procedures and product or service offerings. There is a great deal of uncertainty about how parts of the organization will react to these changes, with a high degree of ambiguity and risk. Transformational change is radical in nature, requiring a shift in the assumptions made by the organization over how it conducts itself and how others perceive it. Incremental or tactical change is where improvements are made to what already exists, leading to a clear scope and low levels of ambiguity.

Figure 1.1 Transformational change process

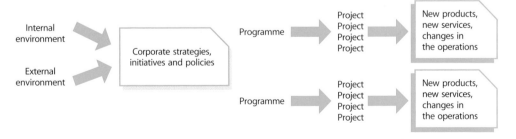

From this description of transformational change, it is clear that programmes are closely tied to the strategic direction of the organization (see Figure 1.1). The organization's corporate strategies, initiatives and policies are influenced and shaped from both the internal and the external environment. Programmes are then defined, scoped and prioritized to implement and deliver the outcomes required.

Programmes in turn initiate, monitor and align the projects and related activities that are needed to create new products or service capabilities or to effect changes in business operations. The projects will deliver the required outputs and the programme will implement these outputs into the operational environment, until finally the full benefits of the programme can be realized.

MANAGEMENT STRUCTURE

The link to strategy means that those responsible for leading and directing the programme must have a senior role within the organization into which the programme will deliver change. Each programme will have a Sponsoring Group consisting of senior managers who represent the areas of the organization that will be most impacted by the changes. Depending on the nature of the programme, this Sponsoring Group may be the board of directors, or their direct reports. In a public sector environment, consideration will need to be given to the involvement of political representatives on this Sponsoring Group. Representatives from government or legislative bodies that are driving the change may be appropriate. The Sponsoring Group will be chaired by the Senior Responsible Owner (SRO) (Figure 1.2) and in successful programmes this role works alongside the Programme Manager.

Figure 1.2 Layering of Programme Organization, control and reporting

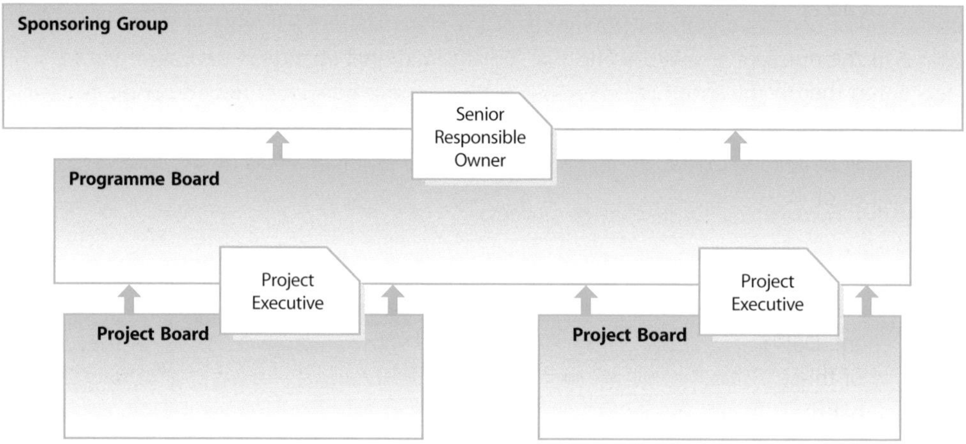

The overriding principle must be that those responsible for sponsoring the programme must be closely tied to those that are responsible for originating strategy and policy. Without this link, there is a danger that the programme will not keep in step with iterations in strategy, and once defined, will continue on a course to deliver the original strategic objectives, rather than the current viewpoint.

In all of these roles, leadership skills are essential, especially the willingness to set direction, influence stakeholders, negotiate a way forward when issues arise and draw together resources from a wide spectrum of interests.

BARRIERS TO ADOPTING MSP

Barriers to successful programme management have a great deal in common with reasons why projects fail. These include:

- Insufficient board-level support
- Unrealistic expectations of organizational capacity and capability
- Insufficient focus on benefits
- Poorly defined or poorly communicated vision of what is to be achieved
- Insufficient engagement of stakeholders.

Insufficient board-level support

Complex programmes require that sponsorship and support come from the very top of the organization, as the failure of the programme has the capacity to threaten the existence of the organization. The outcomes of the programme should be tied to the performance criteria of the most senior roles and should not be delegated to lower levels of management that do not have the authority to implement the scale of change required by the programme. Senior managers will always struggle to find sufficient time to allocate to new initiatives, but if the initiative actually delivers what they are responsible for, then they must accept that it is their responsibility to manage the effort.

Limits on the number of initiatives that an organization undertakes at any one time may be required as there is a natural limit on the amount of change that an organization can cope with at a specific point in time. In some organizations this has been formalized so that a person may hold only one SRO or Programme Manager role at any one time, which limits the number of initiatives to the number of available senior managers.

Unrealistic expectations of organizational capacity and capability

Delivery of the outcomes of a programme will not be undertaken in a static and stable environment. During the life of the programme, the organization will continue to evolve. The pace of this continual and evolving change must be considered when planning the changes that the programme will introduce.

Insufficient focus on benefits

Effort expended on the programme without the delivery of benefits can have serious consequences as the significant resources spent by the organization must deliver a return. Significant initiatives that do not deliver benefits will damage the reputation of the organization in the eyes of its customers and in some cases, the failure of the planned benefits to arrive will lead to the organization going out of business. Failures in delivering benefits within the public sector are addressed by voters at election time.

Poorly defined and communicated vision

The vision for the programme must be forward looking and compelling, drawing support from all those who are impacted by its implementation. It is also important to ensure that the vision makes clear what the programme will not deliver, so that ambiguity is removed. Any ambiguity can be dangerous as it encourages the inclusion of initiatives that whilst beneficial in their own right are not contributing to the outcomes to be delivered by the programme. This is a version of 'scope creep' which can damage the chances of the programme delivering within a 'reasonable' timescale and budget.

Insufficient engagement of stakeholders

Stakeholders will be impacted by the changes that result from the programme and those who are impacted either as users or customers or as suppliers and partners will have the responsibilities for changing their ways of working. Their support, therefore, is of paramount importance. Without it, the changes will not be made, and the benefits of the programme will not be realized.

Sufficient support and realistic expectations rely on commitment and inspired leadership by those originating the programme and by those who go on to sponsor it throughout its life. Focus on benefits, stakeholder engagement and well-defined vision requires a structured approach to programme management, with a comprehensive set of steps to identify the desired outcomes and benefits and communicate these to stakeholders.

BENEFITS OF ADOPTING MSP

A number of benefits are associated with the adoption of MSP. These benefits are felt at the three levels of activity to which the Principles of MSP are applied: the organization as a whole entity; the programme itself; the projects that comprise the programme. The benefits include:

- Effective coordination of effort across the organization as a whole, as the strategic direction is applied in a clearly defined manner to all interested parties. This minimizes the chance that areas of weakness will develop in any one part of the programme, or that factions with their own agendas will lead the programme off course.
- Programmes require commitment of considerable resources by the organization, often over a lengthy period. The application of MSP can reduce the risk that these resources are used in undirected effort, where outputs are produced but do not realize benefits. The emphasis on the identification, management and realization of benefits minimizes the risk of misapplying or wasting resources.
- Application of best practice can minimize the risks associated with incorporating suppliers and partner organizations into the programme, as the methodology by which the programme will be managed can be easily communicated and adhered to.
- As the structure is well understood, time can be spent on what is to be achieved, and not on the manner by which it will be achieved, thus saving time at initiation of the programme and throughout its duration.

- By acknowledging that a structured methodology is being used, the business will feel a greater amount of control is being exercised over the team.
- Projects are only initiated with the approval of the Programme Manager, and they are originated via an analysis of the Blueprint of what is required, and an evaluation of the Benefit Profiles to ensure that the project will lead to or enable the creation of one or more benefits.
- There is a reduction in the opportunity for projects to fail to deliver their outputs as the direction that the Project Executive provides is supported by the monitoring and support activities of the programme team, especially in the areas of risk management and Issue Resolution. Where projects come under pressure due to resource constraints the programme can provide a valuable source of support by reallocating resources across the Projects Dossier to ensure completion.

Governance Themes

2

2   Governance Themes

Within an organization, governance is the control framework on which every aspect of how the organization is managed, directed and controlled is based.

Within a programme, a governance structure will need to be established that not only incorporates this organizational framework but also addresses the specific needs of the programme. In MSP, governance has been grouped into nine key Themes which are explained in this chapter and set out in Figure 2.1 under the simple headings of:

- **What** is the vision of the programme and what future will the programme deliver?
- **Why** is the programme worth undertaking?
- **Who** will be involved in the programme, either within the programme team or as stakeholders impacted by the programme?
- **How** will the programme undertake key aspects of work including plans, risk and issue management and quality management?

Figure 2.1 MSP Governance Themes

What	**Why**	**Who**	**How**
			Planning and Control
Vision	Business Case	Organization	Risk Management and Issue Resolution
Blueprint Design and Delivery	Benefits Realization Management	Leadership and Stakeholder Engagement	
			Vision

ORGANIZATION

What is the purpose?

Whatever the size or level of complexity of the programme, it will require informed decision-making and a management regime that is flexible and likely to be stable over its lifetime.

It is necessary to establish a culture that encourages a flow of information between the projects and the programme and vice versa. To establish this type of culture effectively means that ideas for driving the programme forwards are welcomed from across all of those involved and when problems arise, effort is concentrated on solving the problem and learning lessons from it, rather than finding someone to blame for the problem arising in the first place.

This type of culture requires senior managers to have great confidence in their own ability to drive the programme and to have sufficient confidence in the members of the programme team, so that they are willing to devolve as much decision-making to them as possible. Managers will develop this confidence as a result of experience, but it can in part be generated by an understanding of their responsibilities and exactly what is expected of them as the programme evolves and moves through its lifecycle.

To achieve this requires clearly defined roles and responsibilities coupled with straightforward reporting lines and appropriate levels of authority so that decisions can be taken at the right level within the programme. Too little authority devolved across the programme will place a burden on the SRO and Sponsoring Group. Too much authority devolved to the projects, however, will make it almost impossible for the programme team to exert any influence over the individual projects.

Reporting lines must add value and not simply be in place as a safety net so that all those involved know what is going on. A useful rule is to question any role that has more than one reporting line and ensure that no role has more than two reporting lines. Instances in which two reporting lines are acceptable are generally when there is a need to keep specialist/technical managers informed whilst at the same time reporting to business managers about when the capability will become available.

Although programmes generally have a longer timeframe than projects, they are still a temporary undertaking, and staff will require reassurance that their programme role supports their career development aspirations. They will also need an understanding of how their programme role will fit with their existing operational responsibilities or, if they are to work with the programme full time, how this new management structure will affect them.

What does this mean?

The organization structure that needs to be established for the programme covers a range of responsibilities including:

- Liaison with those responsible for strategy and direction of the organization as a whole
- Day-to-day running of the programme
- Delivery of benefits and maintenance of business as usual.

Figure 2.2 Senior Responsible Owner and the Programme Board

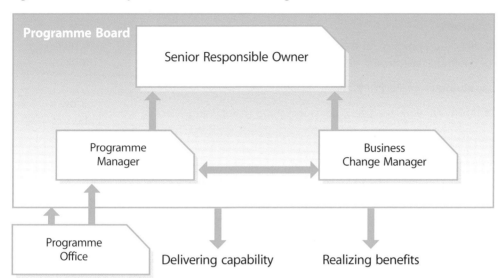

Liaison with those responsible for strategy and direction of the organization as a whole

The SRO is ultimately accountable for the programme and is responsible for enabling the organization to exploit the new environment resulting from the programme (Figure 2.2).

Key responsibilities of the SRO are:

- Owning the vision for the programme and personal accountability for its outcome
- Providing overall direction and leadership for the delivery and implementation of the programme
- Managing the interface with key senior stakeholders, keeping them engaged and informed.

Key attributes of the SRO are:

- Ability to combine realism with openness and the clarity of expression to communicate the programme's vision effectively
- Has the seniority for the responsibilities and accountabilities the role involves, and the experience, character and personality that are right for the programme.

Day-to-day running of the programme

The Programme Manager is responsible for leading and managing the setting up of the programme through to delivery of the new capabilities and realization of benefits.

Key responsibilities of the Programme Manager are:

- Planning and designing the programme and proactively monitoring its overall progress, resolving issues and initiating corrective actions as appropriate

■ Ensuring that the delivery of new products or services from the projects meets the programme's requirements and is to the appropriate quality, on time and within budget

■ Reporting progress of the programme at regular intervals to the SRO and managing communications with stakeholders.

Key attributes of the Programme Manager are:

■ Ability to work positively, developing and maintaining effective working relationships with the full range of individuals and groups involved in the programme

■ Has good knowledge of techniques for planning, monitoring and controlling programmes and projects, including use of PRINCE2™

■ Ability to find innovative ways of solving or pre-empting problems.

Delivery of benefits and maintenance of business as usual

The Business Change Manager(s) is responsible for embedding the new capability into the operational environment of the organization. Although this book refers to Business Change Manager, there may be several Business Change Managers in any one programme, representing the full range of operational areas impacted by the programme.

Key responsibilities of the Business Change Manager are:

■ Implementing the mechanisms by which benefits can be realized and measured

■ Identifying, defining and tracking the benefits and outcomes required of the programme

■ Preparing the affected business areas for the transition to new ways of working; potentially implementing new business processes

■ Monitoring business stability and ongoing capability to cope with the level of change.

Key attributes of the Business Change Manager are:

■ Is drawn from the relevant business areas in order to demonstrate detailed knowledge of the business environment and direct business experience

■ Understands the management structures, politics and culture of the organization(s) involved in the programme

■ Has the management skills to coordinate personnel from different disciplines and the change management skills to bring order to complex situations.

Are there any examples that might help me?

Large organizations often have multiple layers of senior management committees, each empowered to administer an area of the business. In the public sector these management layers are complicated by the need for political representation to be included at decision-making levels. Therefore, whilst it is important to involve knowledgeable and willing participants in the programme organization, this should not be done outside of the 'norms' of the organization.

One local authority who managed this successfully sent its senior management team on a programme management training programme. This enabled the managers to share their expectations of what programme management really meant in terms of workload and day-to-day commitment, and gave them all the same base level of knowledge to carry out their roles. Senior managers were able to see how the programme organization structure 'cut across' many of the existing management committees. This led to a reduction in the number of existing management committees, and enabled the Sponsoring Group to evolve from an existing management committee which had an established pattern of meeting and decision-making which the programme was able to tap into.

Do I have to do this?

Establishment of a clear and effective organization is critical to programme success. Ensuring that the programme organization meets the needs of the programme in its context is an initial and ongoing task that cannot be avoided, or dealt with lightly or done once and then forgotten.

When the programme is first identified and defined, programme roles will be clarified and appointments made to these roles. As the programme progresses and projects are initiated, there will be a further round of appointments at project level. In addition, the programme structure will be evaluated periodically to see if additions or removals need to take place, primarily within the Programme Office and the Change Team(s) managed by the Business Change Manager(s).

What happens if I don't do this?

A programme is a specific undertaking and without the establishment of its own organization structure it will not be given the management commitment and leadership that it requires. The programme is established to deliver a part of the organizational strategy and a vision of what the organization will look like in the future. This requires a degree of objectivity and 'sitting back from' the day-to-day operational issues of the organization, which cannot be achieved if the programme is managed within an existing hierarchical or matrix management framework.

What are the benefits?

By creating a robust and flexible organization structure for the programme, participants will have sufficient experience and authority to:

- Ensure the correct resources are available to the programme
- Influence and engage with stakeholders
- Balance the programme's priorities with those of the ongoing business operations
- Focus on the realization of the business benefits.

Evaluation of each appointment against a comprehensive set of responsibilities will increase the chances that each manager will have the skills required to provide the programme with management of:

- The cultural and people issues involved in change
- Finances and resource constraints and conflicts
- Coordination of projects, the transition to new operational services and the maintenance of the day-to-day business operation.

VISION

What is the purpose?

The vision is the basis for the outcomes that will be delivered and the benefits that will be realized. The vision describes the new services, improved service levels or innovative ways of working that the programme will deliver, and enables stakeholders to engage with and commit to this view of the future.

What does this mean?

An effective Vision Statement will have the following characteristics:

- It is written as a future state, a snapshot of the organization as it will be in the future.
- It is easy to understand and communicate because it does not use any jargon or technical terminology.
- It is written to address the interests of the broadest possible group of stakeholders.
- It describes a compelling future that persuades and convinces the audience that it is a worthwhile undertaking.
- It is motivational and aspirational in its wording, describing a desirable future and encouraging support from all who read it.
- It is believable and relates to the capability of the organization. It does not contain timeframes or other constraints unless they are integral to the delivery of the programme.
- It is short and memorable, often only a paragraph in length, which makes it easier to communicate across the widest possible audience.

Are there any examples that might help me?

There are two main ways in which the vision can be developed. The first approach relies on a carefully selected management team that will draft the vision, paying close attention to the future strategy of the organization. This team will create many iterations of the vision until it fully encompasses the part of the strategy that is to be delivered by the programme. The Vision Statement will then be sent to the board or management committee for approval before disseminating it to a wider audience. This approach works well when strategic direction arises out of a merger or acquisition, where confidentiality is critical.

The second approach involves much wider participation from all stakeholders, who will be asked to participate in workshops where they define their vision for the programme. The SRO and Programme Manager will then evaluate each of these contributions and bring them together as a cohesive vision that the programme team and stakeholders can commit to. This approach works well for building commitment and involvement across a disparate group of stakeholders.

Do I have to do this?

The vision forms the basis of all stakeholder communication and is essential in developing support and understanding for the programme. It is the basis of all other information in the Programme Brief, and is used by those sponsoring the programme to justify that the investment will deliver the strategy required by the organization.

What happens if I don't do this?

Without a description of the compelling future that the programme will deliver, it will not be possible to engage with stakeholders and gain their support for the work of the programme. There is also the risk that all those participating in the programme are working hard to deliver different views of the future, as there has been no formal agreement to the outcomes that they are working towards.

What are the benefits?

The vision clarifies how the future will be different from the present, which enables participants to identify the benefits that their specific area of the business will receive as a result of taking part in the programme.

The vision can build unity and agreement on what is to be done, before the detailed design documents are created. Therefore, when the programme reaches the point of Blueprint creation, all of the stakeholders are in agreement with the 'bigger picture' and can confidently state what will need to be done to achieve it.

As the vision is written in customer-facing terms, technical knowledge is not required to appreciate it or understand it. This ensures an inclusive organization structure, as the programme organization structure comprises staff focused on the business as well as technical specialists responsible for delivery.

LEADERSHIP AND STAKEHOLDER ENGAGEMENT

What is the purpose?

A stakeholder is an individual or group with an interest in the programme, its outcomes and its benefits and dis-benefits.

Effective stakeholder engagement requires well-developed leadership skills. In the context of a programme, leadership is concerned with the meaning, purpose and realized value of the programme. To simplify things, a programme leader concentrates on the What and the Why rather than the How and the When.

These leadership skills will elevate stakeholder engagement past the basic steps of communicating progress and issues, and will acknowledge and address that stakeholders are individuals with their own attitudes, motivation and agendas, operating within their own framework of internal politics. Therefore, as stakeholders are people, attempting to manage them from a purely mechanistic mindset is unlikely to work.

What does this mean?

Whatever approach is taken to stakeholder engagement, care should be taken to allow projects to manage their own communications, wherever this is possible. Too much centralized control of communication can have a demotivating effect on the project teams and cause discontent amongst project-related stakeholders.

However, it is important to ensure that communications are consistent across the programme as a whole, but this might be more the spirit of the messages rather than the actual detail, which can be very project specific.

Figure 2.3 sets out key steps recommended for the Stakeholder Engagement Process, which are then explained more simply in the rest of this chapter.

Figure 2.3 Stakeholder Engagement Process

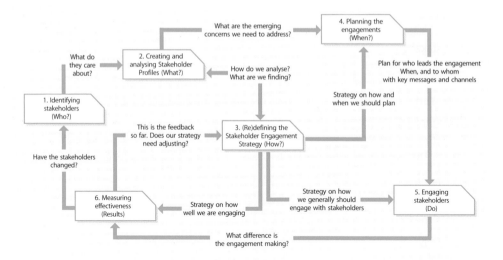

Identifying stakeholders

In this step all the stakeholders involved in or affected by the programme and its outcomes are identified. The Vision Statement and the Blueprint can be used to identify possible stakeholders and this activity must run throughout the life of the programme, as it is unlikely that the stakeholders will remain constant, or will all be identified at the start of the programme.

Where there are large numbers of stakeholders, it can be useful to categorize them. For example:

■ Users/beneficiaries – those that will directly use the outputs from the projects or implement the changes during the transition period

- Governance – management boards, steering groups, audit functions
- Influencers – trade unions, the media
- Providers – suppliers, business partners.

Creating and analysing stakeholder profiles

- Gain an understanding of the influences on and interests and attitudes of the stakeholders towards the programmes outcomes. It is important to recognize that these attitudes may be positive or negative, and that negative stakeholders need as much if not more engagement than those stakeholders with a broadly positive attitude towards the programme.
- Gain an understanding of the importance and power of each stakeholder. Examine the amount of influence a stakeholder has over the outcomes of the programme, and their level of interest in what the programme will deliver. For example, although a patient has a great deal of interest in the modernization programme of their local hospital, they have little power to determine the outcomes of the programme.

Stakeholder analysis must not be conducted as a one-off effort, as the interests and attitudes of stakeholders will evolve during the life of the programme. Failure to review the needs of stakeholders at regular intervals may allow concerns to develop or opportunities for support to be missed.

Identify and create relevant communication options for each stakeholder

The Communications Plan should be defined and implemented as early as possible within the life of the programme, so that a broad base of support and commitment can be developed. The Communications Plan should answer the following questions:

- What are the objectives of each communication?
- What are the key messages?
- Who is the communication intended to reach?
- What objections is the stakeholder likely to have, and how can we address these?
- What information will be communicated and to what level of detail?
- Who will carry out the communication and when will this be done?
- What mechanisms will be used for the communication?
- How will feedback be encouraged, and what will be done as a result of the feedback?
- How will feedback be recorded, reviewed and resolved?

Measuring effectiveness

Stakeholder communication is not one-way, and feedback must be encouraged so that the effectiveness of individual communications and the methods of communication can be reviewed.

Are there any examples that might help me?

Whilst it can be useful to categorize stakeholders, sticking too rigidly to the original interests that are deemed relevant for them can be dangerous. An organization planned a high-profile programme to standardize working practices across a workforce that had evolved from the original organization and two acquired companies. It was decided that the main interests of the trade unions were the reworking of employment contracts, pay scales and working hours. Other initiatives related to career development, training opportunities and management 'fast track' schemes were communicated directly to staff and not to the trade unions. This was a missed opportunity to gain the support and endorsement of the trade unions and enlist their help in 'selling' the initiatives to the staff. Therefore, even though these initiatives were well funded, the initial level of support from staff was not high, as they could not see the relevance of the initiatives to their existing roles.

Do I have to do this?

Stakeholders have a vital role in implementing changes to the operational environment and adopting new ways of working. Without their support, the programme will not be successful. This support will only be gained by relevant and timely communication of the issues that are most relevant to each stakeholder. This is achieved by a structured approach to identification and profiling of, and communication with, stakeholders.

What happens if I don't do this?

Without a systematic approach, it is likely that there will be two key failings:

- Wrong messages are communicated to the stakeholders.
- Stakeholders are not properly identified. Individuals are labelled as stakeholders of the programme when they are not, whereas some stakeholders are not identified, and therefore not communicated with.

What are the benefits?

Stakeholders become an effective, positive and supportive additional resource on the programme and related projects, rather than being an obstacle that must be overcome.

BENEFITS REALIZATION MANAGEMENT

What is the purpose?

A benefit is the measurable improvement resulting from an outcome which is perceived as an advantage by a stakeholder. The changes that a programme brings about will lead to benefits as well as dis-benefits, which are negative outcomes. The programme will also generate side effects and consequences, which can lead to even more dis-benefits. However, if the side effects and consequences are carefully managed they may lead to additional benefits.

The programme must manage benefits, dis-benefits, side effects and consequences to ensure that ultimately what is delivered will be perceived as beneficial by the stakeholders.

To achieve this, Benefits Realization Management:

- Ensures that the projects and activities that the programme intends to carry out are aligned against the Blueprint so that the intended benefits will be realized
- Defines what a 'fit for purpose' capability means, so that the programme will only deliver capabilities that will deliver benefits
- Aggregates the achieved benefits, the expected benefits, costs to date and expected costs against the Business Case to ensure that the programme remains viable
- Provides the Benefits Realization Plan, to track the achievement of the benefits
- Manages risks and issues that may impact on the ability of the programme to deliver benefits
- Identifies adjustments to governance that must be undertaken at end of tranche and benefits reviews to ensure benefits will be realized.

What does this mean?

There are a number of well-thought-out steps that will take the programme through the lifecycle of benefits management, from identification and ongoing management through to realization.

In some cases, identifying benefits is straightforward and obvious. Cost cutting or revenue generation targets that are identified as part of the strategy for the organization will be taken up by the programme as benefits to be realized.

Another method for identifying benefits is to select the relevant key performance indicators (KPIs). KPIs are quantifiable measurements of the improvement in performing an activity which is critical to the success of the business.

The benefits generated by the programme may not be directly measurable as they are intangible or hard to define (e.g. improved reputation for honesty when dealing with customers, or improved environment in which to work). Although these benefits can be captured, they will need to be developed into a more tangible form before they can be measured. Improved reputation for honesty can be further developed into an assessment of the number of times the organization has done what it promised to do when handling a customer enquiry, and improved working environment can be represented by levels of staff turnover, which can be measured by the number of resignations.

In some programmes it is not possible to identify all of the outcomes that the programme will deliver, and therefore it is not possible to fully identify all of the benefits that will be realized. If this is the case, it is helpful to model all of the known outcomes and try to identify the relationships between these outcomes, possible side effects, consequences, new outcomes that had not previously been identified, and benefits and dis-benefits that will result from the outcomes. During the modelling session there is no need to clarify which contribution is a benefit or an outcome; the team should just be allowed to have a free flow of ideas. In this way, creativity will not be stifled and more ideas will be generated. Figure 2.4 shows how this model fits together.

Figure 2.4 Path to benefits realization and strategic objectives

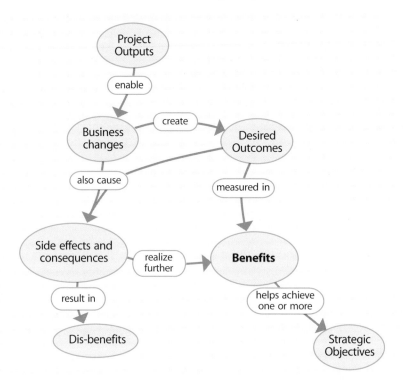

Managing benefits is a complex part of programme management. It is often hard to manage a benefit in isolation from other benefits as there are so many interdependencies between them. Therefore, once benefits have been identified, it is important to map them against each other to identify:

■ Linkages and dependencies between the benefits
■ An understanding of when in the lifecycle of the programme the benefit is likely to be realized.

Once both a benefit and any dependencies have been identified, a detailed description of the identified benefit should be created, called a Benefit Profile. A successful Benefit Profile should pass four critical validation tests:

■ Description – what precisely is the benefit?
■ Observation – what verifiable differences should be noticeable between pre- and post-programme implementation?
■ Attribution – where will this benefit arise? Can the programme claim its realization? A benefit that is likely to be realized as a result of multiple organizational changes should not be claimed as a programme benefit.

- Measurement – how and when will the achievement of the benefit be measured?

Each benefit needs to be 'owned' by an appropriate individual who must be accountable for its successful delivery. The characteristics of the owner are:

- They are affected by the benefit, i.e. it occurs in their area of operational responsibility. Where a benefit crosses operational boundaries, the manager responsible for all impacted areas should be selected as the owner, otherwise it will be easy for more junior managers to avoid their responsibilities for the realization of the benefit by blaming lack of action or effort on the other, related department(s).
- They have sufficient authority within the organization to initiate changes to support the realization of the benefit. A benefit cannot be owned by a staff member too junior to make the changes necessary for its realization. For example, if the benefit is cost savings based on the redundancy of data input clerks who are to be replaced by a new scanning system, the owner must have the authority to make redundancies.
- They have a personal interest in the realization of the benefit, because it has been linked to their annual performance targets and will form part of their annual performance appraisal.

Once a detailed description of the benefit has been created, select the time frame in which it is to be realized. This time frame will be a result of several factors, including:

- The timescales required for the projects that will deliver the outputs needed to realize the benefit
- Linkages and dependencies with other benefits that need to be realized before or at the same time as this benefit
- The need to generate quick wins for the programme, and therefore schedule benefits as early in the life of the programme as possible.

Benefits will need to be measured using the measurements of the 'old' performance of the impacted area of the organization, versus the 'new' measurements. These measurements may need to be taken repeatedly over a period of time, as the benefit might not be fully realized for a number of months or years.

The Benefits Realization Plan is a complete view of all the benefits, their dependencies and the expected realization timescales, including the timing of reviews to formally assess that the benefits have been realized.

The need for the programme to demonstrate that it is making a positive contribution to the organization may affect the scheduling of the projects and activities within the Programme Plan, and the timing of the realization of benefits on the Benefits Realization Plan.

Many programme teams grapple with the dilemma that senior managers who perform the role of SRO or are a member of the Sponsoring Group are not in that role for the long term, due to promotions and resignations. This cycle is speeding up and puts pressure on the programme team to deliver quick wins. Another reason for this pressure is the link between realization of benefits and annual staff appraisals. If senior managers are paid by results, they will be keen to ensure that the programme makes a contribution to the financial success of the organization within 12 months. Figure 2.5 summarizes the steps involved in the management of benefits realization on a programme.

Figure 2.5 Benefits Realization Process

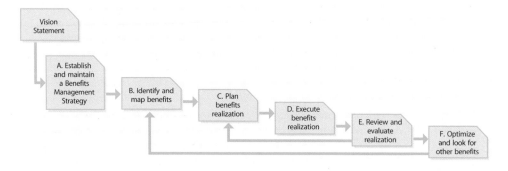

Are there any examples that might help me?

To get started, it is always a good idea to find a benefit that is:

■ Of interest to as many senior managers as possible
■ Simple and straightforward to measure
■ Already being measured within the organization so that additional reporting mechanisms do not need to be introduced.

For example, if staff turnover within the organization is perceived as high, it is of interest to senior managers as it indicates weakness within the structure of the organization. Staff turnover is measured on a regular basis, and there is plenty of data to provide a detailed Benefit Profile. Any programme which includes training and development projects would claim reduction in staff turnover via a fall in resignations as a benefit of the programme.

Do I have to do this?

Realizing the benefits is the main driver for organizing the work into a programme in the first place, so Benefits Realization Management is a key part of MSP.

What happens if I don't do this?

Without this structured approach, it is easy to focus solely on the delivery of the multiple outputs from the projects within the programme and the changes that these will make to the operation. Therefore, change will occur, but it might not be beneficial change.

What are the benefits?

Benefits Realization Management breaks a complicated concept into easy-to-follow steps with clear outlines for the documentation that needs to be produced at each step. It also assigns roles so that there is a clear chain of involvement and responsibility for each member of the programme team.

BLUEPRINT DESIGN AND DELIVERY

What is the purpose?

The purpose of the Blueprint is to ensure a cohesive future state, preventing disparate initiatives from being brought together, as such initiatives will ultimately contradict each other and cancel each other out (Figure 2.6). There is a strong link between the vision and the Blueprint.

Figure 2.6 Relationship between vision, Blueprint and Programme Plan

The Vision Statement is a short, memorable statement of the future, whereas the Blueprint is a comprehensive document providing a detailed view of the future state of the organization. The extra detail required by the Blueprint is often created from the results of a gap analysis in which the differences between the current state and the planned future state are analysed and developed into concrete requirements of what must be put in place to achieve the vision.

It might not be possible to envision all of the details of the future state of the organization, as initial concepts will need to be proved or disproved before a decision is taken to continue with the programme. In this case, the Blueprint will be developed in several sections, with each section showing as much as can be predicted about the intermediate state of the organization at the end of each tranche, and in preparing for the last tranche, the view of the organization at the end of the programme will be added.

At the end of each tranche, and when a major change to the programme is proposed, the definition, scope, delivery status and expected benefits of the programme need to be revisited, which may lead to revisions of the Blueprint. Any lessons that have been learnt during the tranche will be applied to the Blueprint to maximize those areas that have worked well and to eliminate or reduce those areas that have not realized sufficient benefits.

The two tests that are carried out on the Blueprint at this time are:

- Prior to transition – the Blueprint for that tranche of the programme is checked to ensure that the capability described in the Blueprint is ready to be delivered by the transition activities.
- After transition – the operational environment is checked to ensure that the new capability that has been delivered has actually enabled the improvements and the benefits that are expected.

What does this mean?

To gain a comprehensive view of the future, Blueprint design requires undertaking four key steps:

1 Identifying, describing and measuring the current state
2 Defining possible solutions to improve the future state – this requires creative thinking and can come from anywhere in the organization, as well as from outside consultants and supplier organizations
3 Modelling each solution so that the outputs from each potential project are linked to the outcomes as a whole, which are linked to the creation of specific benefits
4 Optimizing the mix of solutions which will produce the most acceptable Business Case – each solution will have its own costs and timescales and the way forward must be the best possible balance of the costs and timescales against the potential benefits on offer.

The Blueprint is not designed in isolation. The Business Case must be developed in parallel with the Blueprint to ensure that the mix of processes, organizational structure, technology and data requirements in the future state is the optimum mix for realizing the benefits. Benefits realization cuts across all programme activity and the Blueprint must be focused on the benefits that will be produced. As each part of the future state of the organization is described, it will trigger the identification of the projects that will deliver the outputs required. This means that the design of the Blueprint will lead to the development of the Projects Dossier, which in turn will lead to the creation of the Programme Plan.

It is important to recognize that it is not always possible to design a complete Blueprint for the programme during programme definition, and that there will need to be a delay as the results of early work of the programme are evaluated. Early tranches of the programme might deliver 'core' changes with later changes building on that core. This provides quick wins, and as each change is smaller it reduces the risk.

Are there any examples that might help me?

A simple way to start writing the Blueprint is to take one section at a time. For example, if the main effect of the programme is to increase the focus on customer service, statements about the intended organization structure might be the easiest to articulate. Working with the Human Resources (HR) Director, the programme staff would define a suggested structure, number of employees, levels of management and descriptions of main roles. Although this would remain only a suggestion, it can then be used as the starting point for defining the processes that staff would undertake, or the systems and office accommodation that they would require.

By defining the Blueprint in this way, it provides senior management with a clear route by which they can develop their ideas. In addition, each section can be cross-checked and fully examined as the next section is developed.

Do I have to do this?

The Blueprint is a model of the organization, its working practices and processes, the information it requires and the technology that supports its operations. It forms the basis for modelling the potential benefits that the programme will realize and enables the creation of a comprehensive Projects Dossier. Without the Blueprint, it is not possible to define the projects that will form the programme, and the vision will remain an idea of how the future will look without any concrete plans for how this will be delivered.

What happens if I don't do this?

Without a carefully considered Blueprint design, the programme will not be able to establish a cohesive Projects Dossier as there will not be sufficient detail in the Vision Statement to cross-check that the projects are required. It will also be impossible for the programme team to make a case for acquiring responsibility for projects that are already underway within the organization but should be managed within the programme structure as they are essential to the delivery or one of more parts of the Blueprint.

What are the benefits?

If the design of the Blueprint is carried out in an inclusive manner, the stakeholders will be involved from an early point in the life of the programme and will have an opportunity to establish a future organization structure that will deliver the benefits that are relevant to their area of operation.

A comprehensive approach to gap analysis during the design of the Blueprint will help to produce plans that encompass the true ability of the organization to manage the scale of the change, rather than delivering an unattainable set of requirements.

By developing the Blueprint in conjunction with the Business Case, the need to realize benefits will guide the structure of the future organization.

PLANNING AND CONTROL

What is the purpose?

This Governance Theme is actually two separate sets of activities. Programme planning delivers the picture of how the programme is going to work on a day-to-day basis. Programme control identifies all of the supporting activities that will be carried out throughout the programme lifecycle.

Figure 2.7 shows an example programme schedule, indicating the grouping of projects into tranches, which leads to the application of controls including end-of-tranche and benefits reviews.

Figure 2.7 Example programme schedule

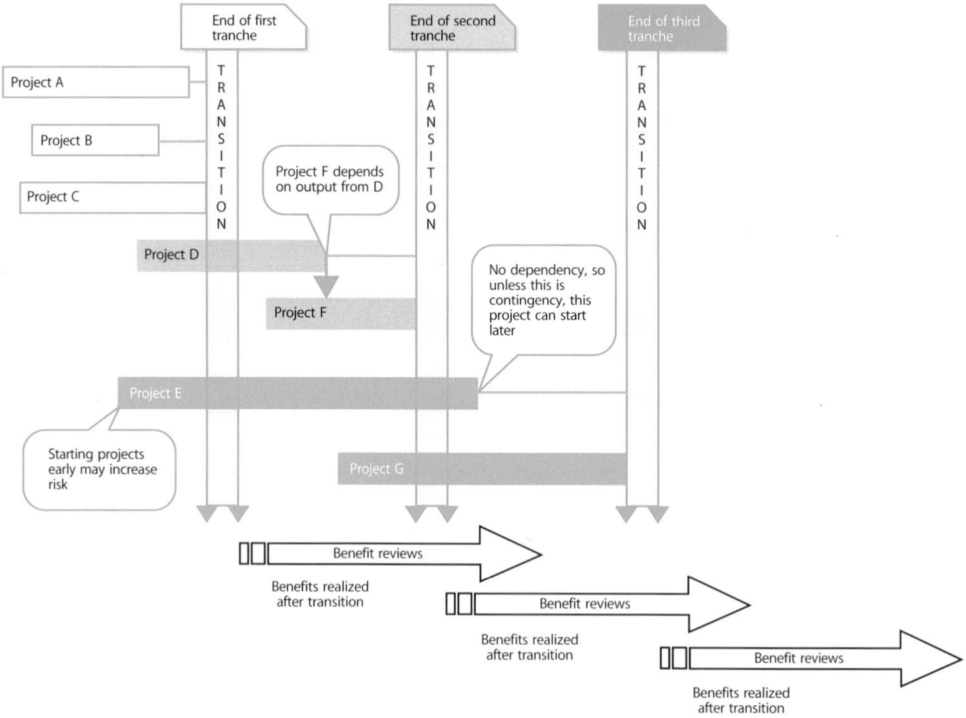

What does this mean?

The Programme Plan includes the following core information:

- Projects Dossier – including project timescales, costs, outputs and dependencies
- Risks and assumptions
- Schedule – including tranches
- Transition plans
- Monitoring and control activities
- Performance targets.

The Programme Plan cannot be created in isolation. It is not possible to schedule any of the projects unless the dependencies that each project has to the other projects and to the benefits that are to be realized are understood. Therefore, the Programme Plan must be developed with reference to the Benefit Profiles and the Benefits Realization Plan, which will outline which projects deliver which benefits and how much time is required for the transition activities associated with each benefit.

An additional layer of complexity that must also be considered before scheduling can take place is resource availability. Human resources, other physical resources such as materials and accommodation, and financial resources will all have a constraint on them, a maximum level above which they are not available. Therefore, the Programme Manager may not be able to schedule all of the projects that would ideally take place at the same time, simply because there is insufficient resource to work on them at the same time.

Transition plans are created by the Business Change Manager(s) and will typically cover three areas of work:

- Pre-transition
- Transition
- Post-transition.

The Blueprint can rarely be delivered in a single pass; it will typically be reached through progressive refinements or step changes in the capability of the organization. Tranches will be identified and set out on the Programme Plan which represent step changes in capability.

Programme controls need to be established so that the right level of information is communicated between the projects and the programme at a sensible frequency. Too much control exerted by the programme team over the projects will lead to demotivated Project Managers, who feel unable to run their project on a day-to-day basis without consulting the programme team over their every move. Too little control leaves the programme team with insufficient project information to take decisions about the dependencies between the projects and identification of risks and issues that can affect more than one project.

Are there any examples that might help me?

An example of an inappropriate level of programme control is where a Project Manager reports to a Project Board that does not contain any programme team members. The Project Manager provides this board with highlight reports on a weekly basis, as the Project Board believes the project is of sufficient risk that it requires close scrutiny. The programme team also feels the same way, but demands a different style of report, also weekly, to be sent to the Programme Office. In addition, the members of the Programme Office ask to meet the Project Manager every two weeks to review the Project Plan and Risk Log. In this situation, reporting can take up a disproportionate amount of the Project Manager's management time and they can feel overly controlled by the Project Board and the Programme Office.

Do I have to do this?

Projects need to be empowered if they are to deliver their outputs, with the project team having sufficient authority to manage the project day to day but operating within clear limits so that they do not exceed time, cost, scope and quality boundaries that would affect other projects within the programme. At the same time, the programme team will require consistent progress information delivered at timely intervals to ensure that the programme is on course to deliver the required capability that will allow for the realization of the planned benefits.

What happens if I don't do this?

Unless a framework for controlling the information flow between the projects and the programme team is established, it will not be possible to compare like with like. Projects run using different approaches and methodologies will create differing levels of detail in their reports, which the Programme Office will then have to ratify before developing an overall picture of the programme.

There is also the danger that changes in strategic direction that have an impact on the objectives of the programme will be inconsistently applied across the different projects in the programme.

Control must be exercised at the programme level as the individual outputs from each of the projects within the programme must function as a whole. Individual project controls will not address this, as one project will not be able to exercise sufficient authority over other projects without intervention from the programme team.

What are the benefits?

Application of comprehensive planning and control procedures will deliver a number of benefits, including:

- A Programme Plan that evolves the level of detail that it contains, as analysis is carried out and the Blueprint and Projects Dossier are created
- A clear understanding of where resources are shared across more than one project, and where there are likely to be resource constraints that may affect the ability of the programme to adapt to changes and requests for additional outputs
- Effective monitoring of the projects within the programme, and a detailed understanding of progress of the programme at any point in time
- Motivated and committed projects teams, with appropriate levels of authority to manage their projects successfully with the support of the programme team.

BUSINESS CASE

What is the purpose?

The Business Case is an aggregation of specific information about the programme:

- Value of the benefits
- Risks to achieving the benefits
- Costs of delivering the Blueprint
- Timescales for achievement.

The Business Case provides the justification for the initial investment in the programme and is evidence of the ongoing viability of the programme. Although it is likely that there will be a business case for each project, these should not be confused with the programme Business Case. The programme Business Case is more than a summation of these project-level business cases, as it includes the costs of changes to the operational environment and the costs of benefits realization.

What does this mean?

The Business Case is actively maintained throughout the programme. It is continually reviewed and updated with new information on benefits, costs and risks at key points during the life of the programme (Figure 2.8). These key points include:

- Creation of the Programme Brief (Identifying a Programme) – the identification of anticipated benefits and estimated costs and timescales in the Programme Brief is actually an outline Business Case, providing the formal basis for assessing whether the investment is viable before committing to the detailed programme definition work
- Creation of the Blueprint (Defining a Programme) – this enables greater understanding of the benefits likely to be realized by the programme, which can then be rolled into the Business Case
- End-of-tranche activities – updating the Business Case to reflect the actual costs of completing the projects and carrying out the transition activities
- When an exception occurs – the Business Case must be updated with the impact of significant issues
- Confirmation that the Business Case has been satisfied – this takes place as part of Closing a Programme.

Figure 2.8 Genesis of a programme Business Case

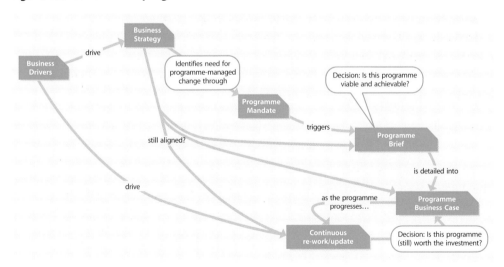

Are there any examples that might help me?

One of the biggest mistakes that the programme team can make is to forget to include the costs associated with transition and benefits realization. This is in part due to the connection between programme management and project management, where the emphasis on the programme becomes biased towards project activity, as it is this that the Programme Manager drives, rather than transition and benefits realization activities which are driven by the Business Change Manager. These costs can become embedded in the budgets of the operation rather than being drawn out into the programme Business Case. This is a serious error, as the costs of transition are usually a high proportion of the programme costs.

Another cost omission is often failure to financially plan for temporary resources required in the operational environment to replace staff who have been seconded to projects within the programme. Added together with the costs of benefits realization, nearly half the programme costs can be missing from the Business Case. Clearly this will alter the perception of the viability of the programme and will allow programme activity to be approved when the programme's total cost indicates that it is not justified.

Do I have to do this?

It is not sufficient to rely on the business cases of each of the individual projects as these will not provide an overview of the viability of the programme as a whole. In fact, in many programmes, each project business case will be extracted from the overall programme Business Case.

What happens if I don't do this?

Without a programme Business Case it will be difficult to select the optimum mix of projects and activities within the Programme Plan. This is because each piece of work has its own costs and associated benefits and can be achieved in different ways depending on how quickly or how cheaply it is to be delivered. Creation of an overall picture of the costs and benefits of the programme allows the SRO and Programme Manager to identify where additional financial resources are to be placed and where resources can be minimized and still achieve the outcomes of the programme.

What are the benefits?

The establishment of a programme Business Case will allow the organization as a whole to ensure that it does not over-commit its finite resources. A programme will require a great deal of resources across its lifetime, and it is important to establish that the resources are available not only now, but will continue to be available until the close of the programme. This is especially important in organizations where there is a great deal of change, as it is often the resources required to maintain business as usual that come under the greatest pressure. The ability of a programme to deliver its outcomes and realize benefits will be compromised if the outputs of its projects cannot be integrated into the operational environment in a reasonable timeframe.

As the programme progresses, the Business Case plays a vital role in ensuring the continued viability of the programme. The impact of all changes must be fully understood before they can be authorized or rejected. These include:

■ Strategic changes or changes to the business drivers that led to the programme in the first place

- Revised benefit and cost estimates from the Business Change Managers and Project Managers
- Any major new issues or risks that are identified.

RISK MANAGEMENT AND ISSUE RESOLUTION

What is the purpose?

Successful programme management must tolerate and manage uncertainty, complexity and ambiguity. Risk Management and Issue Resolution are the vehicles for achieving this. A risk is an uncertain event which if it occurs will have an effect on the achievement of objectives. An issue is an event that has happened, which was not planned and is currently affecting the programme in some way. It must be actively dealt with and resolved.

What does this mean?

Programme risk management is responsible for providing a cost-effective risk management process that includes a series of well-defined and visible steps. The aim is to support better decision-making through a good understanding of what 'might' happen as well as what is planned to happen.

There are nine principles of programme risk management:

- Understand the context of the programme – understand the overall picture of what the programme is to achieve and the areas of the organization and its external partners, suppliers and customers who will be affected. It is useful to perform SWOT (Strengths, Weaknesses, Opportunities and Threats) and PESTLE (Political, Economic, Social, Technological, Legal, Environmental) analyses to identify possible risk areas.
- Involve the stakeholders – failure to include all stakeholders increases the risk that objectives are not fully endorsed prior to the work of the programme commencing, leading to change requests later in the lifecycle of the programme.
- Establish clear programme objectives – risks are directly related to the objectives. Therefore, any attempt to identify and manage risks prior to agreement and sign-off of the objectives will be wasted effort.
- Develop the risk management approach for the programme – the objectives of the programme are unique to that programme. Therefore, this uniqueness should be factored into the way in which risks are identified and managed. Objectives that are linked to the survival of the organization will require closer scrutiny and risk management than objectives that are tied to improving the working environment.
- Report on risks regularly – the usefulness of risk reporting is directly linked to how current the report is. If the structure allows a week for drafting and editing a report before the risks are seen by the Programme Board, this will severely limit the actions it can take with regard to the risk. Risk reporting should be tied to programme activities as it is from these activities that many risks will be derived. For example, when projects enter the testing phase, risks can be identified associated with the failure of the components being tested.

■ Define clear roles and responsibilities – risk management activities will not take place unless they are embedded in the responsibilities of each member of the programme team. Members of the Programme Board should have responsibilities associated with the leadership and direction of the risk management effort, and the Programme Manager and Project Managers should have responsibilities associated with the day-to-day control and reporting of risks.

■ Establish a support structure and a supportive culture for risk management – the programme must establish a culture of trust where participants are not afraid to raise concerns about risks and the ideas for managing the risks are openly shared.

■ Monitor for early warning indicators – for certain risks, it may be possible to establish limits which if breached will automatically trigger pre-agreed actions. For example, if the programme is heavily reliant on external suppliers, limits for the number of late deliveries can be agreed, and if these are breached, action will be taken against the supplier.

■ Establish a review cycle and look at continual improvement – as the programme is likely to have a timescale of several years, the programme team should be encouraged to adopt a cycle of 'continuous improvement' in the way in which risk management policies and procedures are used.

Unlike risks, issues usually require immediate action, as they have already happened. Issue resolution should allow for this timely intervention, preventing the issue from threatening the programme's achievement of its objectives. This intervention usually means a change to the programme will need to be considered; therefore, issue resolution is closely tied to the programme's change control process.

It is likely that there will be a high volume of issues affecting the programme; therefore, prioritization of the issues is important. This can be greatly assisted by the establishment of prioritization criteria, such as:

■ Cost impact
■ Time delay
■ Damage to the reputation of the organization
■ Impact on the scope of the programme
■ Impact on the realization of benefits.

Those issues that cannot be resolved by using the existing resources or those that will impact on the overall delivery schedule of the programme or the delivery within budget or the realization of benefits should be escalated to senior management for resolution.

At programme level, risks and issues can originate from any of the stakeholders or interested parties, or can be identified by those within the organization who are responsible for strategic direction and organization-wide objectives (Figure 2.9). However, there are two important levels of risk and issues that will need to be managed in a systematic and consistent manner if they are not to destabilize the programme environment.

Figure 2.9 Sources of risks and issues at the programme level

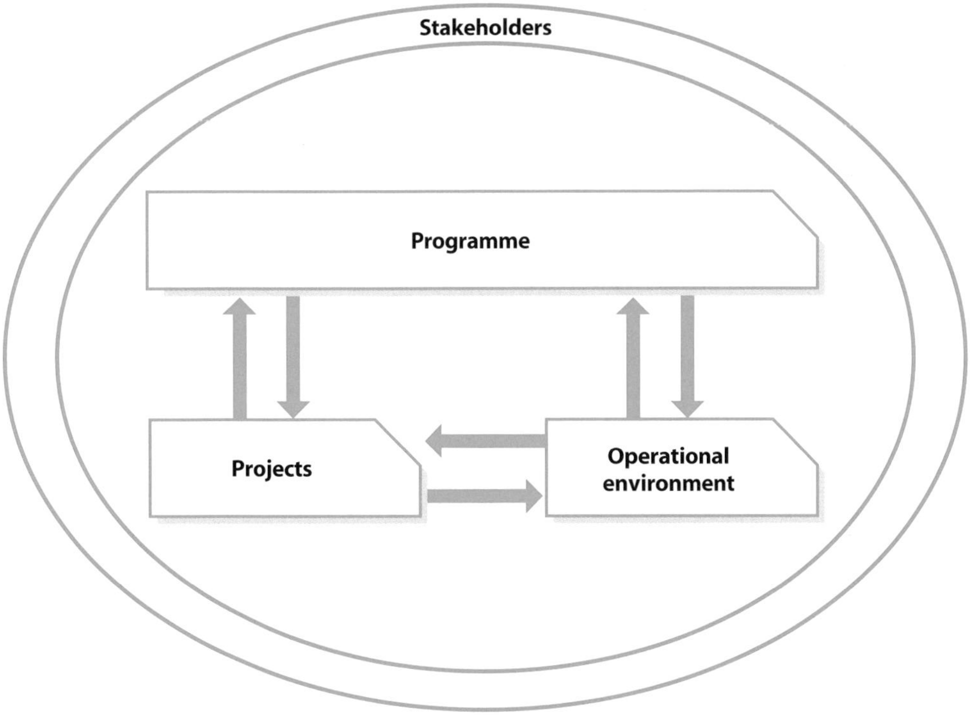

Firstly, risks and issues can be escalated from individual projects, where the Project Manager or Project Board identifies that the risk either will have a significant impact on the delivery of the project or may have an impact on the delivery of other projects within the programme. Secondly, the programme team may identify programme-wide risks and issues which must be communicated to the affected projects, where action can be taken directly by the Project Manager(s).

Are there any examples that might help me?

The greatest difficulty for the Programme Manager is to provide guidance to the Project Managers and Project Boards about those risks and issues that need to be escalated to the programme team. Although it is relatively straightforward to issue guidance which states that those risks and issues which breach a certain cost or time threshold must be escalated, identifying those risks and issues which have an impact on other projects within the programme can be complicated. This is because it is difficult to provide projects with sufficient information about all of the other projects and workstreams within the programme without causing information overload.

An IT company with a large number of inexperienced analysts and programmers overcame these problems by investing time in a large-scale risks and issues workshop during the process of Defining a Programme. Many project staff were invited to join the programme team to identify risks and discuss actions for managing them. They also developed proposals for change control, to be put to the SRO for approval. This gave project staff an opportunity to understand the different projects that were planned to take place and gain real insight into the interdependencies on the programme. As a result it was much clearer which risks were 'single project' and which risks had the potential to affect multiple projects and therefore should be escalated to the programme team.

Do I have to do this?

Risk Management and Issue Resolution are integral to effective programme management.

What happens if I don't do this?

Without these controls, there is a good chance that the programme will be sent off course by an unplanned event and, if action is not taken in a timely manner, the programme may no longer be viable.

What are the benefits?

Managing the risks and issues across the programme will significantly enhance the ability of the programme to deliver its planned outcome and realize its benefits. The programme team has a great deal of knowledge about the wider implications of risks and issues to convey to individual Project Managers, and lessons learned on one project in how to handle these unplanned events can benefit all other projects within the programme.

QUALITY MANAGEMENT

What is the purpose?

Quality management ensures that stakeholders are satisfied that their planned benefits have the best chance of being realized. If quality is not being applied effectively then the assets and the outputs of the programme are less likely to be fit for purpose, which will reduce the chances of the planned benefits being realized. Therefore, achieving quality is an integral part of all the day-to-day activities of the programme (Figure 2.10).

Quality management at a programme level is less easy to define than at the project level, where the outputs of the project must meet the acceptance criteria defined for them. At the programme level there is a need to ensure that the strategic goals of the programme are in line with the strategic goals of the organization as a whole. Quality management applies corporate policies to the programme and ensures that the programme, including the Blueprint and the schedules, remains aligned to these policies.

Figure 2.10 How quality in a programme ensures best use of resources

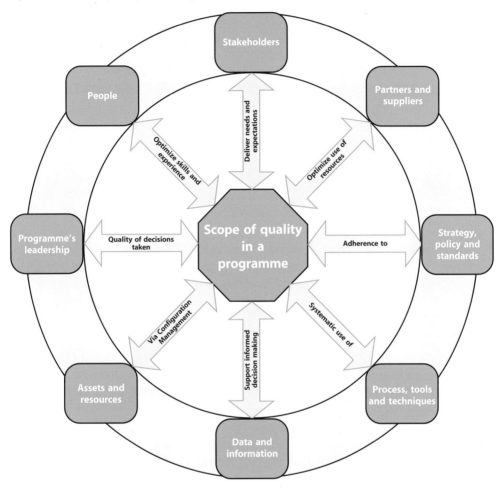

What does this mean?

To identify the key areas that really matter within the programme, you should establish Critical Success Factors (CSFs). These are the limited number of areas that, if fully addressed, will ensure successful completion of the programme. By communicating what these CSFs are, you can ensure that all participants are focused on the areas and activities that are most important.

To help achieve the established CSFs, quality management will need to be applied to a number of different aspects of the programme, primarily:

- Stakeholder relationships – quality assurance activities must ensure that stakeholders are satisfied with the communications process and that the relationship between stakeholders and the programme remains strong.
- Leadership – application of quality management must ensure that effective leadership is taking place, providing clear direction to those inside and outside the programme,

and establishing a governance framework with adequate levels of control.
- Involvement of people – quality management should ensure that people assigned to the programme understand:
  - Their degree of accountability and authority
  - The prevailing policy, processes and standards to which they must adhere
  - What resources are available, including facilities, equipment and materials
  - Their rights to create, access, use or delete data, information and records.
- Adherence to strategies, policies and standards – quality activities need to ensure that the planned changes continue to be correctly aligned to the relevant parts of an organization's strategy and policies. The quality standards, laws and regulations that apply to the existing operation must also be evaluated to ascertain their relevance to the changes planned to the operational environment and, where necessary, these standards must be applied to the outputs of the projects, or if necessary the standards will need to be amended.
- Partners and suppliers – quality management has to ensure that suppliers and partners deliver materials and products that are fit for purpose. This is best achieved through supplier relationships that are mutually beneficial, which will increase the speed of response to changing requirements and lead to a more flexible approach in managing these changing requirements.
- Quality processes – controls must be in place to ensure customers receive products that are fit for purpose. This will include establishment of measurable and agreed levels of quality to be attained by projects prior to developing outputs, and quality reviews during and after the creation of outputs to ensure that the products are fit for purpose.
- Configuration management – the purpose of configuration management is to identify, track and protect the assets of the programme. These include all of the outputs produced by the projects and all of the programme documentation. Overall success will come from the satisfactory functioning of a combined set of project outputs and operational functions. As the failure of one component leads to the failure of the whole assembly, processes must be in place to ensure that all individual components are identified and understood, and any changes to them assessed, tested and controlled.
- Measurement and analysis – effective decisions are based on the accurate measurement of data and the analysis of reliable information. Quality management must ensure that there are processes to monitor the quality of the information supplied by the projects and the Business Change Manager(s) in relation to the operational environment.

Are there any examples that might help me?

A company that manages large amounts of data for other companies used a quality workshop to develop a comprehensive approach to quality management within their programme to expand the business across Europe. The company is subject to a strong regulatory framework for the protection and privacy of the data that it holds, and there were concerns that the members of the programme team, many of whom were independent contractors running specific projects, would not be aware of all of the regulations and relevant quality processes that applied to their work. The workshop included key players in quality management from across the company including Internal Audit, Regulatory Compliance, Quality Management, Financial Control and experienced departmental managers.

Do I have to do this?

Quality management is an essential part of programme management, which must run continuously throughout the life of the programme. It affects every aspect of the programme, from the creation of programme documentation to the outputs from the projects.

What happens if I don't do this?

Without a structured approach to quality management, there is the risk that the programme will deliver outputs that, although workable in their own right, do not adhere to the necessary standards of the organization and do not fit with other outputs from the programme. This will lead to a disjointed delivery of new products and services that are not capable of delivering the benefits intended by the programme.

What are the benefits?

Effective quality management will ensure that other programme activities are effective, including:

- Governance – making sure the processes and rules are being followed and are working effectively
- Alignment of the Blueprint with policy and strategy – ensuring that the changes delivered by the programme are still relevant
- Delivering the Capability – making sure project outputs are fit for purpose and that they will deliver the capability that will lead to the desired benefits
- Risks and issues – quality is directly relevant to detecting and managing issues.

Transformational
Flow

3

3 Transformational Flow

Figure 3.1 Overview of the Transformational Flow

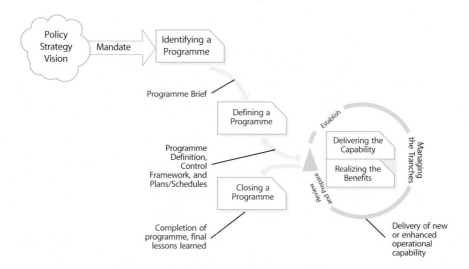

In the earlier part of the book, the Governance Themes demonstrated how the structure of the programme environment can be created. In this section, the Transformational Flow (Figure 3.1) provides a route through the lifecycle of a programme, passing through development and delivery to achieve the outcomes and benefits desired.

The programme achieves its objectives via a series of iterative, inter-related steps. Each of these steps or processes results in documentation, meetings and decision points that manage the programme throughout its life. Some of the processes are likely to be repeated within the lifecycle of the programme, depending on its complexity. This is particularly true of Delivering the Capability, Realizing the Benefits and Managing the Tranches, all of which are repeated for each tranche of the programme.

IDENTIFYING A PROGRAMME

Figure 3.2 Identifying a Programme process – inputs and outputs

What is the purpose of this?

This process develops the Programme Mandate into a more detailed document called the Programme Brief (Figure 3.2), clarifying what is to be achieved and the desired benefits. Creation of the Programme Brief should result in the systematic identification of the:

■ Objectives and vision
■ Required benefits
■ Potential risks
■ Outline costs
■ Timescales.

This identification should also enable those involved to identify any overlap with other initiatives that are planned or are already underway. This is an important step as there is a risk that without this consideration, there will be duplication of effort across the organization, or changes planned by the programme will contradict other efforts being made elsewhere.

Another reason for undertaking this process is to establish who will be involved in sponsoring the programme and taking key decisions throughout the life of the programme. Relevant senior executives will be asked to form a Sponsoring Group. Those chosen should be evaluated against the following factors for their relevance to the programme:

■ Do they have a strategic interest in the programme?
■ Does the programme significantly impact on their ability to deliver their business objectives?
■ Do they have funding or budgetary responsibility for areas covered by the programme?
■ Will the changes created by the programme need to be delivered within their areas of responsibility?

The SRO will be the member of the Sponsoring Group who has ultimate accountability and personal responsibility for the success of the programme. The SRO should be appointed as early as possible as they will provide valuable leadership as well as being a focal point for all those who will be impacted by the programme. This role imposes an additional workload and it is important to establish that the senior manager best suited to become the SRO can actually find time to perform their role. This can be an uncomfortable time as the SRO may have to evaluate their current workload and be prepared to delegate certain responsibilities to others, which can be regarded in highly political organizations as a sign of weakness or disinterest. However, it is essential that the SRO is more than a figurehead, and actually has the time to engage with and lead the programme.

The SRO may find it helpful to establish a Programme Board at this point in the programme to provide additional resource. A fully functioning Programme Board can be very beneficial to the SRO, especially when the workload is high. The Programme Board will assist in the following areas:

- Define the acceptable risk profile for the programme and its constituent projects
- Keep an eye on the programme's ability to deliver on time, on budget and to deliver the agreed benefits
- Resolve issues between the different projects not only to ensure that there is no duplication of effort but also to ensure that no work is overlooked, or that projects do not contradict one another
- Provide assurance that operational stability will be maintained as the projects deliver and their outputs are adopted into business as usual.

It is also important to establish the Programme Preparation Plan which will enable the Sponsoring Group to make an informed decision about committing to the next process, Defining a Programme. This plan should cover:

- The cost, time and resources required to carry out the Defining a Programme process
- How governance can be applied to the Defining a Programme process
- How stakeholders will be identified and engaged during Defining a Programme.

What are the benefits?

Although this process requires some effort, this is minimal in relation to the effort required by the rest of the programme. However, it provides essential information, on which the rest of the programme will be based. It provides an opportunity to explore and if necessary challenge any assumptions that were contained in the Programme Mandate and should generate commitment to the programme through the appointment of the Sponsoring Group and the SRO.

The time spent clarifying the objectives and benefits of the programme often pays dividends later in the lifecycle, as it is easier to challenge and mould where the programme fits into other change initiatives before the work commences, rather than trying to amend work once it has begun. Support for the programme is generated by listening to the views and concerns of others during this process, rather than providing managers with a fully formed idea of what will be done. As with all change initiatives, it is easier to work within an environment of 'doing change to yourself' rather than 'having change done to you', and it is during this process that consultation and exchange of ideas can build that environment.

Do I have to do this?

Defining a Programme is an essential process, as there is insufficient detail in the Programme Mandate to enable senior managers to commit to the programme in full. The concept must be further developed so that an evaluation of the benefits can be made and management commitment given in the form of creation of the Sponsoring Group and the Programme Board.

The Programme Brief will form the basis of future work and its approval provides a firm basis for developing the Blueprint and the Business Case for the programme.

What happens if I don't do this?

If the programme went straight from Programme Mandate to the next process, Defining a Programme, then it is likely that plans will be made to deliver outcomes that are not fully committed to or fully understood in terms of their ramifications for existing work. Also, there would be no understanding of the time and effort required to carry out the process of Defining a Programme, as no preparation plan would exist. Identifying a Programme also provides an opportunity to appoint senior managers to the Sponsoring Group and the Programme Board, without whom the programme would not have the level of commitment and focus that it will require as it moves through its lifecycle.

How do I get to the next step in the process?

Before moving to the next process, ensure that the following steps have been carried out:

- Members of the Sponsoring Group have been identified, and their particular interests and perspectives on the programme have been clarified
- The level of support that each member of the Sponsoring Group will provide to the programme has been identified
- Each member of the Sponsoring Group has confirmed their agreement to their own role and the responsibilities of that role
- The Programme Mandate has been confirmed by the Sponsoring Group
- The Programme Brief has been created
- The Programme Preparation Plan has been created.

What questions should I ask to get to the next step?

- Does the Programme Brief make it clear what the objectives of the programme are?
- Do these objectives tie back to the strategy or corporate plan of the organization?
- Does each operational area impacted by the programme have a representative either on the Sponsoring Group or on the Programme Board?
- Has the SRO cleared enough of their workload to actually fulfil their role?

Who is involved?

Table 3.1 summarizes the roles, tasks, skills and knowledge required for the Identifying a Programme process.

Table 3.1 Roles, tasks and skills involved in Identifying a Programme

Who is involved	Task	Skills/knowledge
Sponsoring Group	Each member of this group first confirms their sponsorship of the programme, by accepting a role in the Sponsoring Group	■ Strategic thinking
	They then confirm their agreement to the information contained in the Programme Mandate	■ Commercial awareness
	The appointment of the SRO is confirmed and any members of the Programme Board who can be identified at this time are also confirmed	■ Judgement
	Finally, approval to proceed to Defining a Programme is given	■ Clear understanding of what it means to provide sponsorship for work that will be carried out across the organization, and potentially outside their areas of responsibility
SRO	Produces the Programme Brief and develops the Programme Preparation Plan	■ Strategic thinking
	In both of these tasks, the SRO may be assisted by a small team or a Programme Office function, if this already exists within the organization	■ Commercial awareness
		■ Judgement
		■ Programme management experience and knowledge – at the very least, an understanding of the programme lifecycle and a commitment to remain in post until completion of the programme
Programme Board	Participates in the production of the Programme Brief and the Programme Preparation Plan	■ Strategic thinking
	Reviews the operational impacts of the programme on their area of responsibility and the raising of concerns and risks to the continuation of business as usual	■ Understanding of the operational structure of the organization
		■ Commercial awareness
		■ Project and programme management knowledge

Are there any examples to help me?

Although there are no confirmed metrics for how long it would be sensible to spend in this process, many organizations have found that typically 5–10% of the timescale of the whole programme will be spent in this process.

A critical concern that a number of organizations have raised is the need to free up the time of the SRO to carry out their tasks. There are three main impediments to achieving this: management teams of organizations are not usually so large that it is possible for other senior managers to take on additional workload; SROs themselves are often unwilling to give up any area of their portfolio as they see it as decreasing their power; and if the SRO does reassign some of their responsibilities, this can take them further away from the decision-making of the organization – which is a disadvantage when it comes to checking that the direction of the programme is in line with the strategic direction of the organization.

An example of how these problems can be overcome is provided by a large investment bank that was preparing for a wholesale change to its operating procedures, and the systems supporting these procedures, as a result of the bank's need to improve its audit trail. The board was presented with five major programmes of work that needed to be completed over the next three years. As a result, a number of senior managers had their responsibilities expanded beyond the point at which they could physically carry out their roles. It was agreed that an additional round of senior management appointments would be made, enabling each SRO to appoint themselves a Business Manager, who would be responsible for day-to-day decision-making across the business line for which the SRO was responsible. The Business Manager reported to the SRO and had some delegated powers of decision-making. This freed up sufficient time for the SROs to carry out their programme responsibilities.

DEFINING A PROGRAMME

Figure 3.3 Defining a Programme process – inputs and outputs

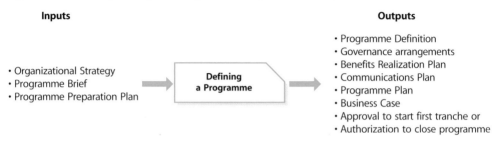

Inputs	Outputs
• Organizational Strategy • Programme Brief • Programme Preparation Plan	Defining a Programme	• Programme Definition • Governance arrangements • Benefits Realization Plan • Communications Plan • Programme Plan • Business Case • Approval to start first tranche or • Authorization to close programme

What is the purpose of this?

The Defining a Programme process carries out the detailed definition and planning of the programme (Figure 3.3), which provides the basis for deciding whether to proceed with the programme or not. The Programme Brief is the starting point, and the Programme

Definition document is the key output of this process. The Programme Definition document will explain:

- What the programme is going to do
- How it is going to do it
- People who will need to be involved
- How it will be controlled
- The justification for going forward.

What the programme is going to do

The explanation of what the programme is going to create or result in is provided by the Blueprint, driven by the benefits required and the capability described in the Vision Statement. It is essential that sufficient time is given to the creation of this document, which often requires a range of resources to be involved to provide business analysis and organizational design ideas. Although time consuming, it is easier to give this work the proper resources at this point in the lifecycle. It is far more complicated to alter the direction of the programme to include additional requirements if they are discovered later than it is to design the programme to take account of these requirements from the start.

How it is going to do it

An outline Programme Plan will be developed showing:

- The estimated timescales for the projects
- An estimate of the duration of the transition period for each tranche, although detailed planning is not practical until sufficient progress has been made in each of the individual tranches
- An indication of when the tranches will occur.

People who will need to be involved

The people who will need to be involved in the programme are the stakeholders who are impacted by the activities of the programme, and a programme team that will manage the programme on behalf of the Sponsoring Group. Staff who may be given specific change management, programme or project management roles later in the programme may be asked to form a small team to support the SRO in defining the programme. This team may have been identified in the Programme Preparation Plan created in Identifying a Programme.

How it will be controlled

The programme will be controlled via the governance arrangements, captured within the programme strategies, which will also to some extent explain how the programme is going to achieve its objectives. This control framework should ideally be compatible with existing corporate governance frameworks, including the frequency of reporting, the units of measurement that are used and the types of analysis that are conducted.

Governance is a constant theme that runs throughout the programme, and the arrangements that are put in place in this process should be clear and concentrate on the actual activities that members of the programme team need to carry out. For example, in Leadership and Stakeholder Engagement the types of communications activity that the programme will conduct should be clearly identified so that plans and budgets can take account of them. A workshop with delegates invited from across the organization will be more time consuming and more costly to arrange than an e-mail newsletter, but it will provide the opportunity for two-way communication.

The justification for going forward

The justification for going forward will be summarized by the Business Case, and further supported by each of the Benefit Profiles. The initial Benefit Profiles are created from the information in the Vision Statement and the Programme Brief. As the Blueprint is designed these can be extended and refined and owners appointed for each benefit.

The Business Case is developed in parallel with the Blueprint. This is because it is important to temper the 'promises' made in the Blueprint against the costs of developing them, to ensure that the end result is positive.

What are the benefits?

The overriding benefit of this process is clarity of direction for the programme. This process allows the Sponsoring Group to be provided with a clear understanding of the activities that will be undertaken at least in the early part of the programme, along with practical steps for the governance of the programme as a whole. There is clarity of what the programme has to achieve, the people who will be involved and the benefits that will be realized.

This process provides an opportunity for the Sponsoring Group to approve the definition of the programme and commit to the development of the future state of the organization contained in the Blueprint.

Do I have to do this?

Yes, this process provides essential information that will be used to manage the programme throughout its life.

What happens if I don't do this?

The programme cannot move forward without a clear understanding of the future state of the organization that it must deliver and the projects that will be required to deliver this future state. The justification for the programme must be developed, showing each of the benefits that will be realized by the programme. No further progress can be made on the programme until this has been done.

How do I get to the next step in the process?

The next step in the process is to begin to deliver capability and realize benefits through the initiation of the projects outlined in the Programme Plan. Therefore, to start the first tranche, it is essential that all programme resources are now in place, and staff have been fully briefed on their roles. The Sponsoring Group will decide at the end of Defining a Programme if there is sufficient justification to moving forwards, and if this is not the case, the Group will take action to close the programme.

What questions should I ask to get to the next step?

- Have stakeholders been involved in the creation of the Blueprint and the Business Case?
- Has more than one round of Blueprint design taken place, to ensure that the best mix of future state, projects and benefits has been created?
- Is there evidence that the resources are available to deliver the Programme Plan?
- Has the Projects Dossier been validated against the Blueprint to ensure that all project outputs will deliver only the future state, and not additional outputs that, whilst beneficial, lead the programme away from the realization of its planned benefits?

Who is involved?

Table 3.2 summarizes the roles, tasks, skills and knowledge required for the Defining a Programme process.

Table 3.2 Roles, tasks and skills involved in Defining a Programme

Who is involved	Task	Skills/knowledge
Sponsoring Group	■ Approves to proceed at the end of the process	■ Strategic thinking
		■ Commercial awareness
		■ Judgement
SRO	■ Responsible for establishing the team that will carry out the definition of the programme	■ An understanding of the interdependencies of the different parts of the programme definition, without which the SRO will not be able to test the assumptions that the team has used when specifying the best mix of future state, projects and benefits that the programme can deliver
Programme Manager	■ Establishes the programme infrastructure	■ Experience and training in programme management
	■ Develops the Vision Statement and Blueprint	■ Understanding of the strategic direction of the organization
	■ Designs the Projects Dossier	■ Commercial awareness
	■ Identifies the tranches (with the Business Change Manager)	■ Problem-solving skills
	■ Designs the organization structure	■ Negotiation skills
	■ Designs the governance arrangements	
	■ Develops the Programme Plan	
	■ Confirms the Business Case	
Business Change Manager	■ Models and validates the benefits and develops the Benefit Profiles	■ Understanding of the strategic direction of the organization
	■ Identifies the tranches	■ Commercial awareness
	■ Identifies the stakeholders	

Are there any examples to help me?

One of the dangers during the creation of the Blueprint is the emergence of different factions within the organization with their own agendas and demands, which they may attempt to have included in the programme, even though their inclusion is not essential to the realization of the planned benefits. In this case, it is essential that the SRO has the support of the Sponsoring Group in rejecting calls to include work that has not been addressed elsewhere in the annual budgets and plans for various departments.

An SRO who successfully demonstrated this approach undertook his own research on the contents of the corporate plan for each department for the coming year, and identified ahead of his first meeting with the Sponsoring Group where the points of conflict were likely to lie. After the meeting, he explained that his research had enabled him to see where work had been included in the corporate plans that had insufficient budget but with some links to the programme. He correctly identified that in order to get sufficient funding for these pieces of work, members of the Sponsoring Group would try to tie them to the programme. Therefore, he identified why they were not relevant, or in what ways the work would duplicate effort made in the programme, and successfully fought off their inclusion. Equally, he was able to identify two pieces of work that required inclusion in the programme as independent management of this work would have created an unacceptable level of programme risk (risk of late delivery and risk of delivery of insufficient quality).

MANAGING THE TRANCHES

Figure 3.4 Managing the Tranches process – inputs and outputs

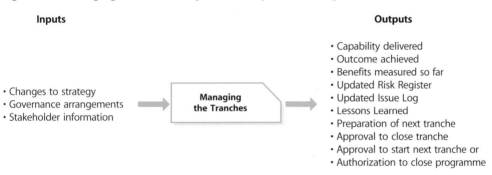

What is the purpose of this?

A tranche is a group of projects that deliver step changes in capability and realize benefits. Managing the Tranches (Figure 3.4) 'wraps around' the processes of Delivering the Capability and Realizing the Benefits, and ensures that throughout each tranche the governance arrangements, which define how the programme is set up, managed and controlled, are in place and are operating effectively. There are four main tasks that this process carries out:

- ▪ Preparation work to establish the tranche
- ▪ A set of activities that assure the effective delivery of the current tranche
- ▪ Preparation of information and activities that will be used in the next tranche
- ▪ Activities to close this tranche, once all of the outputs have transitioned successfully.

Preparation work to establish the tranche

Each role within the programme must have a clearly defined set of responsibilities that each individual understands and accepts. Those associated with the programme may require training in the tools that the programme is going to use, including planning tools, document management software, and financial accounting and other reporting systems.

The physical environment that the programme will occupy must also be established, including office space and facilities such as access to meeting rooms, access to systems and telecommunications.

Effective delivery of the tranche

The Risk Register and Issue Log will need to maintained, and the overall profile of the level of risks and issues monitored. After the initial risk assessment of the tranche, action should be taken to ensure that the level of risk starts to decline. Once the tranche moves into transition, the majority of open risks will be related to transition, as nearly everything else would have been completed and closed off. Issues will increase as quality assurance activities take place. As transition approaches, the number of open issues should decrease. It is important to monitor this profile and ensure that any deviation from this expected pattern is investigated and actioned where necessary.

Stakeholder communication will take place throughout the tranche to ensure that they are kept informed and engaged in the work of the programme. The programme team must ensure that there is two-way communication between themselves and the stakeholders as misunderstandings can cause significant problems.

The Blueprint and the strategic objectives of the organization must remain aligned. The programme team must check for any changes to the strategic direction of the organization and carry out an impact assessment on the programme. The team must also check that the projects within the programme or the direction of the programme overall has not drifted off course, delivering outcomes that do not fully align with the intended strategy.

Configuration management must be applied, to track each new item as it is created, and to track any changes to existing items. The contribution of configuration management to the smooth running of the tranche will develop as the tranche develops, due to the volume of products created by the projects and the programme team.

There are points during the tranche when particular pressure will be applied to the available resources. For example, as a project nears its completion, testing and training activities may require resources from the operational environment to be removed from their day-to-day roles to become the test team for the project. As the tranche nears completion, operational staff may need additional staff as the ways of working are changed, and the productivity of each member of staff slows whilst they adapt to the new environment.

Preparation of information for the next tranche

In preparing information for the next tranche, it is important to learn from this current tranche. In applying what has been learnt, adaptations to the governance framework (strategies) and the organization structure may be required. In addition, there may be a need to refine the Blueprint, Benefits Map, Benefit Profiles and Projects Dossier.

Activities to close this tranche

The main activity to close the tranche is a review meeting, which must assess the ongoing viability of the programme and ensure that the delivery options and strategy remain optimal. This review will be led by the SRO and is likely to include presentations from the Programme Manager and the Business Change Manager.

What are the benefits?

The process provides valuable management activities which the programme needs to ensure that the work being conducted by the projects and operational environment is actually taking place. Without this process it would be too easy to concentrate on Delivering the Capability, with its emphasis on creating outputs from each project, without looking at the wider picture of risks, issues, progress reporting, auditing, procurement and contracts. The same can be said of Realizing the Benefits, which concentrates on measuring benefits without having the wider view of the progress reporting and resource management.

Do I have to do this?

Yes, this is the process that is operated on a day-to-day basis by the Programme Manager and the Programme Office to ensure that everything that is stated in the Programme Plan is actually taking place.

What happens if I don't do this?

This process provides a critical monitoring function for the programme, and without it there is a good chance that the programme would fail to deliver outputs from all of the projects within the tranche in an organized way, and that transition would not be carried out in a structured format that minimizes disruption to the operations of the organization.

How do I get to the next step in the process?

This process continues until the end of the tranche, and begins again at the start of the next tranche. Therefore, progress to the next step relies on a successful conclusion to the end-of-tranche review.

What questions should I ask to get to the next step?

- Have the plans, definition, management strategies and Business Case for the next tranche been refined and developed based on lessons learned so far?
- Have baseline measurements for each of the areas where benefits are expected been taken, and were performance measurements taken after transition to see if there has been an improvement?

Who is involved?

Table 3.3 summarizes the roles, tasks, skills and knowledge required for the Managing the Tranches process.

Table 3.3 Roles, tasks and skills involved in Managing the Tranches

Who is involved	Task	Skills/knowledge
Sponsoring Group	■ Initiates compliance audits	■ Understanding of the quality management framework of the organization and the programme
SRO	■ Initiates compliance audits	■ Understanding of the quality management framework of the organization and the programme
Programme Manager	■ Establishes the tranche	■ Risk management skills
	■ Delivers the tranche	■ Change management and issue resolution skills
	■ Closes the current tranche	■ Understanding of the procurement process and the specifics of each contract that is drawn up with each external supplier
	■ Prepares for the next tranche	
Business Change Manager	■ Measures benefits realization	■ Change management skills
	■ Maintains business as usual	■ Use of configuration management information from the Programme Office to ensure all staff are using the most up-to-date processes and products as they become available from the programme
Programme Office	■ Maintains information and asset integrity	■ Change management and configuration management skills
	■ Transition to stable operations	■ Commercial awareness

Are there any examples to help me?

A good example of resource management comes from a large airline that was running a programme to replace its booking systems. As we can all appreciate, passengers do not tolerate delays in airports very well, and there was concern that any changes to working practices that would slow the booking staff would cause unacceptable check-in queues. Therefore, the training programme for these staff needed to be comprehensive, which meant that they would be unavailable for check-in duties. The programme team saw this as a significant risk to day-to-day operations very early in the tranche, and took action to secure the services of recently retired staff on short-term contracts to cover the training period. As these staff had recently retired, they were already familiar with the existing booking systems and processes of the organization and did not need a lengthy induction and training programme of their own. Their contribution enabled large numbers of existing check-in staff to be trained in the new systems so that the productivity dips associated with transition were minimized.

This example shows how transition activities to adapt to the new processes and products produced by the programme must be planned as carefully as any of the project effort that delivers the new processes and products.

DELIVERING THE CAPABILITY

Figure 3.5 Delivering the Capability process – inputs and outputs

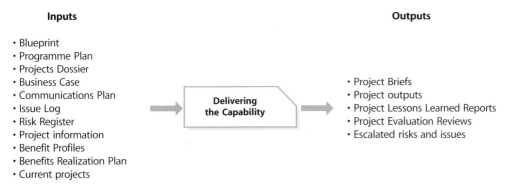

Inputs		Outputs
• Blueprint		
• Programme Plan		
• Projects Dossier		
• Business Case		• Project Briefs
• Communications Plan	**Delivering**	• Project outputs
• Issue Log	**the Capability**	• Project Lessons Learned Reports
• Risk Register		• Project Evaluation Reviews
• Project information		• Escalated risks and issues
• Benefit Profiles		
• Benefits Realization Plan		
• Current projects		

What is the purpose of this?

The Delivering the Capability process (Figure 3.5) is dedicated to the management of each of the projects that form each tranche of the programme. This process is repeated for each tranche and ensures that each of the projects listed in the Projects Dossier delivers outputs that enable the creation of the capabilities outlined in the Blueprint.

Delivering the Capability works in tandem with the process of Realizing the Benefits, and overall guidance for both processes is provided by the process of Managing the Tranches.

Essentially, Delivering the Capability carries out three main tasks for each of the projects:

■ Starting the projects
■ Monitoring the projects
■ Closing the projects.

As many projects are running simultaneously throughout the tranche, the programme team is carrying out these three tasks at the same time but for different projects. Therefore, there needs to be an organized and structured approach by the Programme Office at all times so that the Programme Manager knows the status of each of the projects of the tranche at any time.

Starting the projects

The Programme Manager is responsible for commissioning each project. A Project Executive (Sponsor) and a Project Manager is appointed for each project, and a Project

Brief is supplied by the programme team. There is no need for a Project Mandate as creation of the Projects Dossier has removed any uncertainty about the general idea of the project, and the outputs, timescales, resource requirements and dependencies with other projects have already been established. Therefore, this information can be captured and refined in the Project Brief.

It is the responsibility of the Programme Manager to ensure that each project management team understands the Project Brief and the standards for project management that the programme expects from it. Key areas that the Programme Manager should explore include:

■ Explanation of where the project fits into the timeline of the programme and the projects that will be running concurrently with it

■ Identification of all dependencies that this project has with other projects that are just completing or will complete after the outputs from this project are completed

■ An explanation of the areas of the organization that will be directly impacted by the creation of the outputs from the project, and an explanation of how these outputs will be implemented into the relevant operational areas

■ An explanation of the governance structure of the programme, especially the communications responsibilities to stakeholders and the reporting responsibilities to the Programme Office

■ Identification of the escalation route that must be followed for risks and issues.

Monitoring the projects

Each project needs to be monitored by the programme team to ensure that it is on course to deliver what the programme needs. The Project Manager, and to some degree the Project Executive, are monitoring that a project will deliver its outputs on time, within budget and to the level of quality required by the users. The programme team has a wider responsibility, to ensure the project remains aligned with the direction of the programme. Changes to the direction of the programme may occur as a result of:

■ Changes in strategic direction of the organization

■ Changes to the legislative environment in which the organization operates

■ Changes as a result of non-delivery by other projects.

Aside from alignment with programme objectives, the progress reporting from each project must address:

■ Updates on the accuracy of time and cost estimates contained in the Project Plan

■ Confirmation that sufficient resources are in place to carry out the work defined in the Project Plan

■ An overview of changes that have been made to the scope or quality criteria of the outputs

■ Details of any assumptions that the project team is relying on to carry out its work

■ Overview of the levels of risks and issues for the project.

Each project must also be aligned with the benefits that are related to the project's outputs. This means that throughout the life of the project, there must be structured reviews of the relevant Benefit Profiles to ensure that the outputs are likely to deliver the desired benefits. These reviews can be incorporated into key milestones for the project such as the end of each stage, and the knowledge of the Business Change Manager will be particularly important in spotting any discrepancies between what the project is planning to deliver and what the operation will need to create the benefits.

The risks associated with each project must be actively managed, and issues must be resolved. Tolerance levels should be established so that the majority of risks and issues can be handled by the project team, and only exceptional items escalated to the programme team. The procedures that the Project Manager must follow will be set out in the Project Brief, but the Programme Manager must monitor this situation via the progress reporting to ensure that anything that could affect the programme as a whole is being addressed.

Stakeholders must be engaged throughout the life of each project. There is a general responsibility to keep stakeholders informed of progress and to maintain their levels of engagement with the programme. However, there are also specific responsibilities associated with the delivery of the capability. Without the involvement of stakeholders in each of the projects, the projects will fail to deliver the required outputs. Stakeholder involvement is required in the following situations:

- Capturing the needs of the stakeholders in the requirements analysis
- Reviewing the designs with the stakeholders
- Participation of stakeholders in testing, quality reviews and training in use of the new outputs.

Closing the projects

As each project prepares for closure, there must be a formal handover of the outputs to the programme. A post-project review should also be planned to assess the realization of benefits from the outputs of each project. Lessons learned from the project should be disseminated across the programme.

What are the benefits?

This process controls each of the projects that form a tranche of the programme. In controlling the start of the projects, there is greater certainty that the projects understand exactly what the outputs must be, and will therefore have a more structured exchange with the stakeholders in gathering the specific requirements for the outputs and getting sign-off of the intended design of these outputs. By controlling the progress of the projects, the programme creates monitoring activities which provide a useful proactive approach to discovering risks and issues that may affect other projects or the programme as a whole.

Do I have to do this?

The programme must control the projects as they are the main vehicle by which the programme will deliver step changes in capability and realize benefits resulting from the implementation of the project outputs.

What happens if I don't do this?

Without formal management of each of the projects that form the tranches of the programme, it will be difficult to ensure that the outputs are relevant to the vision of the programme, and that they will be delivered to the required level of quality within a budget and timescale that enables all other aspects of the programme to be completed.

How do I get to the next step in the process?

This process continues until the end of the tranche, and begins again at the start of the next tranche. Therefore, progress to the next step relies on a successful conclusion to the end-of-tranche review. At the end of the last tranche, the process of Closing a Programme will be the next step.

What questions should I ask to get to the next step?

- Has each of the projects delivered the expected outputs to the required level of quality?
- Has delivery of the outputs from this tranche been in line with planned costs and timescales?
- Has each supplier delivered outputs in accordance with their contract?
- Has the Programme Office established lessons learned about this tranche, for dissemination to Project Managers and other stakeholders?

Who is involved?

Table 3.4 summarizes the roles, tasks, skills and knowledge required for the Delivering the Capability process.

Table 3.4 Roles, tasks and skills involved in Delivering the Capability

Who is involved	Task	Skills/knowledge
Programme Manager	▪ Initiates projects	▪ Experience and training in programme management
	▪ Monitors projects throughout their lifecycle	▪ Understanding of the strategic direction of the organization
	▪ Closes projects and disseminate lessons learned to other parts of the programme	▪ Commercial awareness
	▪ Engages stakeholders	
	▪ Aligns projects with benefits realization	

Are there any examples to help me?

A programme is formed of many projects, and it is important that this process is carried out consistently for all of the projects, otherwise problems can arise where one project team has a greater understanding of the context of its work than another project team within the same programme, and so portrays the benefits of what is being created inappropriately.

An example of how this can be resolved comes from a software development company where the Programme Office developed a 'project initiation process' that was applied to each project within the programme. The process included the template for the Project Brief, and all other templates of project documentation, a project management training course for all project staff, which explained the method that the company used for its projects, a set of programme documentation and a copy of relevant strategic documents setting the context of the programme. It was a simple idea that worked very well and saved time, because the Programme Manager could brief the team on specific areas of the project, knowing that all other relevant documentation had already been passed to the team by the Programme Office.

REALIZING THE BENEFITS

Figure 3.6 Realizing the Benefits process – inputs and outputs

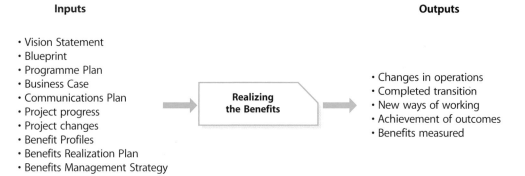

Inputs

• Vision Statement
• Blueprint
• Programme Plan
• Business Case
• Communications Plan
• Project progress
• Project changes
• Benefit Profiles
• Benefits Realization Plan
• Benefits Management Strategy

Realizing the Benefits

Outputs

• Changes in operations
• Completed transition
• New ways of working
• Achievement of outcomes
• Benefits measured

What is the purpose of this?

The Realizing the Benefits process (Figure 3.6) is dedicated to the identification, management and successful realization of each of the benefits associated with the programme. This process runs throughout each tranche of the programme and ensures that the transition from the old to the new ways of working does not adversely impact on the stability and performance levels of the operation.

Realizing the Benefits works in tandem with the process of Delivering the Capability, and overall guidance for both processes is provided by the process of Managing the Tranches.

Essentially, Realizing the Benefits carries out three main tasks throughout a tranche:

■ Managing pre-transition

- Managing transition
- Managing post-transition.

During each tranche, multiple projects will be delivering outputs which must be transitioned into the operational environment. The Business Change Manager will need to review if these can be achieved in a single change to the operation, or will need to be achieved through a series of incremental or modular changes.

Managing pre-transition

Before transition takes place, the Business Change Manager will need to establish a Transition Plan, containing all of the activities that will take place during transition. This plan usually contains a greater level of detail than the Programme Plan, and is similar in levels of activities to a Project Plan. Key activities that the Business Change Manager will need to plan for are:

- Establishing the detailed responsibilities of those staff:
  - Responsible for maintaining the business operations during the transition
  - Responsible for undertaking work using the new ways of working
- Identifying additional activities that will need to be carried out to ensure that the business is fulfilling operational requirements during transition (e.g. the running of additional reports or additional reviews and checks on the work)
- Identifying activities that need to be suspended during the transition, either because there are insufficient staff to carry them out, or because they run contrary to the activities that are taking place in transition
- Exit or back out arrangements that will be required if the change fails badly and the old ways of working need to be restored.

To ensure that the benefits can be realized according to the Transition Plan, the Business Change Manager must realistically assess the operation's appetite and readiness for change. Key points that will need to be covered are:

- Recent track record and experiences of implementing change and this type of change in particular
- Availability and willingness of skilled resources to take part in a change initiative
- Support for this change from suppliers and customers. If either of these parties is unhappy with the current level of service that they experience, their willingness to move to a new way of working is unlikely to be high
- How much this change will affect the culture of the organization and 'the way we do things around here'. A significant change will take longer and need a great deal more support than a more straightforward change to systems and processes.

Before transition takes place, the Business Change Manager will need to measure the current situation. The specific areas of the business that are to be measured were specified in the Defining a Programme process, when the Benefit Profiles were created. However, it is during this process that these measurements are actually taken. The challenge for the

Business Change Manager is to ensure that these measurements can be undertaken by the available resources without interfering with the day-to-day operations of the organization. Unfortunately, measuring the current state can require a great deal of effort, so it is important to establish measures that are relatively easy to put in place, or preferably are part of the existing corporate reporting process.

Whatever is measured, the information that is produced should pass the following tests:

- Currency – the data must be current and ongoing. Old data only represents the organization as it once was, not how it currently is
- Accurate – if the information is unreliable it is likely to lead to invalid decisions being taken. Where possible, data should be cross-checked with a second source
- Relevant – measuring too many items can lead to information overload and critical conclusions not being drawn.

Before and during transition, the Business Change Manager must monitor progress of the projects to ensure that the outputs are on course to deliver the required benefits. Designs and prototypes should be assessed to see how likely they are to work in a full-scale operational environment. This allows the Business Change Manager to consider the question: Will the scale of the improvement be enough to produce the desired benefits? This answer to this question may lead to changes at the project level. Another area that will need to be monitored for possible changes is the current operational environment. This should be assessed to ensure that it will be ready to accept the outputs from the project and, if necessary, adjustments will need to be made. For example, if the current operation is unstable due to the resignation of key staff members, or if transition activities in other parts of the organization have caused delays and confusion, then the timetable for transition will need to take account of this.

This is a great deal of work, and Business Change Managers are unlikely to work in isolation. A Change Team may be created, representing the interests of the parts of the organization to be changed. The remit of this team is to ensure that these parts of the organization are appropriately involved and thoroughly prepared for the transition.

Communication to all those affected must begin prior to transition. If communication is left too late there will be significant resistance to the changes, which may lead to limited participation by staff or active refusal to take part in the transition. Disenfranchised staff will work hard to maintain the current operational environment, or return to this environment once the changes have been implemented, which will undo all of the work achieved in transition, reducing or eliminating the realization of any benefits.

Managing transition

Transition is formed of three key steps:

1 Initiate transition – as the projects approach completion, the relevant business operations must be notified. They should ready themselves for transition by:
    - Finishing off any outstanding pieces of work

- Physically reorganize the office or production line
- Order new equipment, materials or stationery
- Make room for new equipment
- Set up temporary facilities for additional staff.

The Transition Plan should provide a route map to follow during this period.

2 Enact transition – transition can start as soon as the SRO, in consultation with the Programme Board, has given approval to start. This approval will be based on confirmation from the Business Change Manager that the following actions have taken place:
- All outputs from the relevant projects are complete
- Operational staff are trained in their new roles
- There are no outstanding risks or issues that the operation is unwilling to accept
- Contingency and back out arrangements are in place.

3 Review transition – at this point the project team can be disengaged, and the transition reviewed for any lessons learned. The new ways of working will require a settling down period, and embedding these new ways of working into 'business as usual' starts at this point. Until this has occurred, benefits cannot be fully realized. Communication with the stakeholders will concentrate on the success of the new ways of working, but must be carefully handled so that claims about the levels of benefits achieved are not declared too early in the process.

Managing post-transition

Old systems and working practices must be decommissioned. If the old ways are not dismantled it provides an opportunity for the organization to slip back to how things used to be done, instead of maintaining the momentum achieved during the transition.

What are the benefits?

A comprehensive Transition Plan will clarify when the benefits are likely to come on stream, and this plan must be compared with the Benefit Profiles and Benefits Realization Plan, and adjustments made to ensure all documentation is in line.

At this point, new performance measures must be taken and compared with the measures taken in pre-transition.

During this time the Business Change Manager must be prepared to react and adapt to events as they develop. This means that the situation must be closely monitored against pre-agreed stop/go criteria and action taken where appropriate. Communication with stakeholders on the progress of the transition will be essential for building confidence and ongoing support.

Do I have to do this?

The structure that this process brings to programme management ensures that the identification and ultimate realization of benefits is embedded into every step of the programme. No project will be included unless it is clear what part it plays in realizing the benefits. No transition activities will take place unless they lead to the realization of the benefits. The scope of the programme will be controlled by relating back the activities of the programme to the benefits that will be realized as a result of these activities.

What happens if I don't do this?

Without the emphasis on the need to realize benefits, the programme will not have the desired positive outcomes. Work will be carried out and resources used in the creation of this work, but the focus will be on what is done, rather than on what it will contribute to the organization. This leads to the inappropriate use of resources across the organization, and no organization has an unlimited amount of resource such that they can allow this situation to occur.

How do I get to the next step in the process?

This process continues until the end of the tranche, and begins again at the start of the next tranche. Therefore, progress to the next step relies on a successful conclusion of the end-of-tranche review.

What questions should I ask to get to the next step?

- Has transition completed so that all staff and processes have moved to the new ways of working?
- Have old working practices and systems been dismantled?
- Have measurements been taken of the new performance levels?
- Do the performance measures indicate that benefits have been realized?

Who is involved?

Table 3.5 summarizes the roles, tasks, skills and knowledge required for the Realizing the Benefits process.

Table 3.5 Roles, tasks and skills involved in Realizing the Benefits

Who is involved	Task	Skills/knowledge
SRO	■ Gives approval to proceed with transition	■ Understanding of the operational structure of the organization
		■ Commercial awareness
Business Change Manager	■ Plans, initiates, enacts and reviews transition	■ Strategic thinking
	■ Monitors benefits realization	■ Understanding of the operational structure of the organization
	■ Communicates changes to all stakeholders	■ Commercial awareness
	■ Decommissions old systems	■ Project and programme management knowledge
	■ Monitors and reports on progress	

Are there any examples to help me?

Preparing the operation for the transition activities can be very time consuming and, if not carefully managed, can involve too many staff worrying about what they will be doing next week, rather than concentrating on what they have to achieve this week in their normal roles. An example of this is a simple office move, where the new office is an output of one of the projects of business development programme. As part of initiating transition, staff evaluate their existing workspace to identify furniture, files and equipment that must be taken to the new office, and items that are to be archived or disposed of. By involving all staff, productivity in the current environment will fall. Therefore, it may be better to identify one person who is responsible for undertaking this task on behalf of each team or department in the current office, and who will work with the moving company to relocate the effects and establish the new office environment.

CLOSING A PROGRAMME

Figure 3.7 Closing a Programme – inputs and outputs

Inputs

• All programme information

Closing a Programme

Outputs

• Confirmation of programme closure
• Disbandment of programme team
• Lessons learned
• Plan for post programme benefits reviews
• Results of the programme closure review

What is the purpose of this?

The main purpose of the Closing a Programme process (Figure 3.7) is to ensure that there is formal recognition across the organization that the programme has closed. To enable this to happen, an evaluation will need to take place to provide reassurance that the programme has delivered the required new capabilities that were promised in the Blueprint and that the outcomes have been assessed through a review of the benefits that the programme has realized.

Although it is likely that benefits have been realized throughout the life of the programme, it is important to establish that the majority of benefits have now been achieved, and make provision for measuring any benefits that are due to come on stream after the programme closes.

What are the benefits?

Organizationally it is often easier to allow the programme to continue in existence almost permanently. This is because a great deal of expertise in the changes that the programme has brought has been developed within the programme team, and disbanding of these team members can lead to a loss of knowledge and history. This can be overcome with a structured approach to knowledge management and the full integration into the business of all the outputs from each of the projects.

Closing a Programme allows for the decommissioning of the resources and infrastructure used by the programme. The amount of resources still consumed by the programme at this point may be minimal as the majority of resources are usually associated with individual projects and these will have been reassigned at the end of each project. If the programme structure has remained in place for some time after the closure of the final project, often it is only a few team members and the office that they occupy that remain to be decommissioned.

The main benefit of this process is to allow the organization to acknowledge what has been achieved, and acknowledge how this work has taken the organization forward in delivery of its strategy. It is a useful full stop, allowing senior managers to understand what was required to make this step forward, which enables them to plan more effectively for the next step forward, i.e. the next programme.

Do I have to do this?

Yes, without this process the programme is never fully completed. This process should also be followed if the programme is forced to close before its planned end. There are many reasons why this might occur, including:

- Evidence that the programme is not and will not be able to deliver sufficient benefits to justify the costs
- The organization is not able to secure funding to continue the programme
- External circumstances have changed sufficiently to render the remainder of the programme irrelevant.

What happens if I don't do this?

The value of the programme is not acknowledged, allowing for critics to denigrate any achievements and create an environment in which subsequent programmes will find it difficult to gain the necessary management commitment.

The organization continues to fund a programme management environment when resources could be more effectively applied to the operational environment.

How do I get to the next step in the process?

Although in terms of a specific programme the next step is nothing, as the programme is now closed, it is worth considering what the real next step is. Simply, this is likely to be another programme, as organizations do not stop changing. Therefore, to get successfully to this next step, effort must be given to learning the lessons from this programme and applying them to the next programme. It is worth remembering that, in documenting lessons learned, information previously only relevant to the programme team and those directly involved in the projects of the programme will now become available to a wider audience. Therefore, it is important to review your notes and insert background information where applicable.

In addition, there may be a requirement for a future review to provide a complete assessment of the benefits realized as a result of the programme, including those benefits that were not ready for assessment when the programme closed.

What questions should I ask to get to the next step?

- Are the reasons for the programme closure clearly understood by the stakeholders?
- Have sufficient benefit measures been captured to judge the success of the programme against the Business Case?
- Has responsibility for future Benefit Reviews been assigned?
- Have all remaining resources been reassigned?
- If the programme is closing before its planned end, have all options been thoroughly investigated to make sure it cannot continue successfully?

Who is involved?

Table 3.6 summarizes the roles, tasks, skills and knowledge required for the Closing a Programme process.

Table 3.6 Roles, tasks and skills involved in Closing a Programme

Who is involved	Task	Skills/knowledge
SRO	■ Reviews the programme	■ Understanding of the operational structure of the organization
	■ Confirms programme closure	■ Strategic thinking
	■ Feeds back conclusions from the programme to strategy and policy makers	■ Judgement
Programme Manager	■ Notifies all stakeholders that the programme is closing	■ Communication skills
	■ Updates and finalizes the programme information	■ Team management skills
	■ Confirms ongoing support is in place	■ Understanding of the operational structure of the organization
	■ Disbands the programme management team	
Business Change Manager	■ Confirms ongoing support is in place (in conjunction with the Programme Manager)	■ Understanding of the operational structure of the organization
	■ Ensures the need for any future Benefit Reviews have been identified and responsibilities for them assigned	

Are there any examples to help me?

An experienced programme manager who works for an outsourcing consultancy always ensures that as part of closing each programme, he provides a written summary of the key contributions that each member of the programme team have made to the success of the programme. He handwrites these 'references' and, although they are often a lot of hard work, he does it as he sees it as a personal commitment and thank you to his staff, many of whom are anxious about their next job move and are keen to gain more management responsibility as a result of what they have learnt on the programme. This programme manager has been carrying out this reference service for the past 15 years and, unsurprisingly, does not find it difficult to get staff to commit to joining each new programme he undertakes.

Product
Document
Outlines

Appendix A: Product Document Outlines

In order to apply a consistent approach to programme management, it is helpful to standardize the content and format of the documents that are used. Many organizations develop templates for these documents, and to assist in this process, the content suggested by MSP for the most commonly used documents has been included in this appendix.

As we have shown in this book, programmes vary enormously from each other in scope, duration, risk and levels of activity. Therefore, the headings to be included in each document are only suggestions, and the exact format of each document will vary depending on the programme and individual organizational standards.

Table A.1 Description of documents

Title	Purpose	Physical content
Benefits Management Strategy	Used to establish the approach to realizing benefits and the framework within which benefits realization will be achieved	Measurement methods and processes that will be used to monitor and assess the realization of the benefits
		A description of the functions, roles and responsibilities for benefit planning and realization, aligned with the programme's Organization Structure
		Scope and explanation of which areas of the business will be covered by benefits management enabling and realization activity
		Priorities for the programme in terms of benefit types to be sought (e.g. cashable direct), to inform and focus the filtering and prioritization process
		Any organizational-specific information or headings that should be included in Benefit Profiles
		Tools, systems and sources of information that will be used to enable measurement
		CSFs against which the effectiveness of Benefits Realization Management should be measured
		Clarification of benefits-related terminology appropriate to the organization
		The review and assessment process for measuring benefit realization covering who will be involved in the reviews; how and when the reviews will be carried out

Title	Purpose	Physical content
Benefit Profile	Used to define each benefit (and dis-benefit) and provide a detailed understanding of what will be involved and how the benefit will be realized	Reference number or identifier
		Description of the benefit (or dis-benefit)
		Programme or organizational objectives supported; KPIs in the business operations that will be affected by the benefit, both immediately after realization and for the future
		Current or baseline performance levels, and improvement or deterioration trajectory anticipated
		Other benefits that this benefit contributes towards
		Costs of achieving the benefit that have not been captured in project or other costs, e.g. redundancy costs
		Features required for the benefit to be realized; the project(s) within the programme directly related to the realization of the benefit
		Business changes required for realization (to process, culture, people, policy)
		Earlier benefits on which this depends
		Related issues and risks to the full realization of the benefit
		Any dependencies on other programmes or projects outside the boundary of this programme
		Who owns this benefit (typically the Business Change Manager for this area of the business)
		Who will receive the benefit
		Measurement (financial wherever possible):
		■ Description of the measure(s)
		■ How the measure is to be tracked
		■ 'As is' measure
		■ Target performance/score
		■ From when (improvement begins)
		■ To when (when measurement will cease or when target reached)
		■ Non-project costs associated with realization and measurement.

Title	Purpose	Physical content
Benefits Realization Plan	Used to track realization of benefits across the programme and set review controls	A schedule detailing when each benefit, dis-benefit or group of benefits will be realized (typically as a chart with benefits of the same measure aggregated over time intervals through the life of the programme's Business Case)
		Appropriate milestones for when a programme for Benefit Review of progress could be carried out, to take a forward view of the likelihood of ongoing success
		Dates when specific outcomes will be achieved that enable the benefits
		Dependencies
		Detail of any handover and embedding activities, beyond the mere implementation of a deliverable or output, to sustain the process of benefits realization after the programme is closed
		Could also include the Benefits Map
Blueprint	Used to maintain the programme's focus on delivering the required transformation and business change. A description of the current and changed organization	A schedule detailing when each benefit, dis-benefit or group of benefits will be realized (typically as a chart with benefits of the same measure aggregated over time intervals through the life of the programme's Business Case)
		Processes and business models of functions, including operational costs and performance levels, of the required vision of the future state; may be expressed in a number of ways, and will include flow and process graphics, organizational charts
		Organization structure, staffing levels, roles and skill requirements necessary to support the future business operations. Any necessary changes to organizational culture, style or existing structures and personnel may also be included
		Technology, IT systems, tools, equipment, buildings and accommodation required for the future business operations together with details of re-use of existing infrastructure or implementation of new infrastructure to support the vision of the future state
		The data and information required for the future business operations, together with details of how existing data and information will be changed or redeveloped to provide the necessary requirements for the vision of the future state

Title	Purpose	Physical content
		The complete Blueprint Document contains several sections: the current state, sections for the intermediate future state for each tranche, and the final future state for the end of the last tranche
Business Case	Used to validate the ongoing viability of the programme	The strategic objectives for the programme, reflecting the Vision Statement, and aligning with the organizational context and business environment
		The expected benefits, with recognition of the organization's capability to achieve the necessary transformation and change
		The overall risk profile, indicating the major risks to programme delivery and benefit realization. Detailed risk assessment will be part of the programme's Risk Register
		Estimated costs and overall timescales. Detailed scheduling of programme milestones will be part of the Programme Plan
		Investment appraisal
		Forecasts of cashflow and expenditure over the programme timeline
		Options and approaches that have been considered
Information Management Strategy	Describes how the programme will establish the measures, systems and techniques that will be used to maintain and control programme information	Systems that will be used to store information
		Responsibilities for management and maintenance of information
		Levels of confidentiality to be applied
		How information integrity will be maintained
		Criteria to assess effectiveness (cross-referenced with the Monitoring and Control Strategy)
		Approach to audit
		Scope of the strategy
		Release management arrangements for updated baselines or individual configuration items, and the relationship to the Programme Communications Plan
		Approach to information availability

Title	Purpose	Physical content
		Configuration management and change control procedures, including:
		▪ Configuration management responsibilities and systems and storage arrangements
		▪ Configuration management naming conventions and policies that will be used; these may be adopted from broader organizational policies
		▪ Explanation of how configuration management baselines will be implemented within the programme
		Information security arrangements to maintain confidentiality, integrity and availability of information within the configuration management arrangements
		Standards and processes to cover data and records management
		Use of terms, e.g. policy, strategy – could be a glossary
Issue Resolution Strategy	Used to describe the mechanisms and procedures for resolving issues	How issues will be captured and assessed, and responsibilities
		Process and explanation of how change control will work in the programme
		How exceptions that take the programme beyond its boundary margins will be managed
		How information about their likely impact will be assessed
		Responsibilities for the effective management and resolution of issues within the programme
		How issue ownership will be allocated
		How actions will be identified and by whom; who will carry out and manage the required actions
		Description of how issues will be escalated or allocated between project and programmes
		Criteria for allocating severity ratings to issues. Categories for severity might be 'critical' (that is, adverse effect on the benefits such that continuation of the programme is unacceptable), 'major', 'significant' and 'minor'

Title	Purpose	Physical content
		Definition of what constitutes a project- or programme-level issue
		Categorization mechanism for filtering issues, e.g. technical, business process, organizational, programme process
		How actions will be monitored and evaluated for their effectiveness
		Any organizational-specific heading information that will be required to be recorded in the Issue Log, other than the generic Issue Log template
		Criteria used to assess the effectiveness of issue management within the programme
Monitoring and Control Strategy	Defines how the programme will apply internal controls to itself	Criteria to assess effectiveness
		How projects will be monitored
		How the programme's internal process effectiveness will be monitored
		What standards will be applied to the projects
		What controls will be in place, including decision authority
		Information that will be required for monitoring
		Margins within which the programme will operate
		Escalation routes for managing exceptions, e.g. how do you stop the programme?
		Any links to independent assurance such as gateway reviews
Programme Brief	Used to define the programme objectives and outcomes; this is a snapshot of what the programme is expected to achieve	The information initially referred to as the Programme Brief will evolve into a number of other documents; hence the Vision Statement, Issues Log, Risk Register, Business Case, Benefit Profiles are shown as being created during Identification; at this stage they may be at a very strategic or conceptual level
		Outline Vision Statement for the programme, which will include a description of the capability that the organization seeks from changes to the business and/or its operations. Delivery of this capability is the end goal of the programme

Title	Purpose	Physical content
		Outline description of the benefits or types of benefits that should be delivered from the new capability, an estimate of when they are likely to be achieved, and an indication of how they will be measured. It also includes significant dis-benefits
		Risks to the programme that can be recognized at this point in time, any current issues that may affect the programme, and any known constraints, assumptions or conflicts that may potentially affect the programme. These should also reflect levels of stakeholder support and engagement
		Outline Business Case, with as much detail as is available on the estimated costs, timescales and effort required to set up, manage and run the programme from initiation through to delivery and realization of the benefits. The overall timescale for the programme may be relatively long, perhaps two to five years
		Options for delivery that are known about at this stage
		Programmes will provide an indication of the effort and resources required; an initial listing of the candidate projects or activities required should be included, together with rough timescales and explanation of those that will be terminated
		Assessment of the current state and how the current business operates and performs in the areas that will be impacted by the change
Programme Communications Plan	Sets out the timetable and arrangements for implementing and managing the Stakeholder Engagement Strategy	Description of key messages and programme information to be communicated, and the objectives for delivering these communications
		Responsibilities for delivering key messages and other information about the programme
		Identification of the stakeholder audience for each communication
		Description of channels to be used, including feedback mechanisms
		Process for handling feedback, through a feedback log, how objections will be identified and handled, and including the approach to managing negative publicity

Title	Purpose	Physical content
		Schedule of communications activities, including target audiences for each
		Reference to any supporting project and business operations communications activity
Programme Plan	Used to control and track the progress and delivery of the programme and resulting outcomes	Project information including the list of projects (the Projects Dossier), their target timescales and costs, and the dependency network showing the dependencies between the projects
		Cross-reference to the Risk Register to explain any planning contingencies that have been made to mitigate risk
		An overall programme schedule showing the relative sequencing of the projects
		Explanation of the grouping of projects and major activities into tranches, and the points at which end-of-tranche reviews will take place
		Individual schedules and plans that can be consolidated into the Programme Plan, e.g. Resource, Quality, Information, Benefits Realization, Information, Transition and Communications
		Shows when the outputs from the projects will be delivered to the business and what transition activities will be required to embed the new capability into business operations
		Implementation schedule for the Monitoring and Control Strategy
Programme Preparation Plan	Explains outputs, boundaries and controls from the Programme Definition activities	Resources required and where they will be sourced from
		Boundaries and margins within which the team will work during definition
		Description of the deliverables from definition
		Governance and controls that will be applied to the defining team
		Schedule of activities to achieve the outputs
		Membership of the Programme Board
		Any key members of the team who are already known, e.g. Business Change Managers and Programme Manager

Title	Purpose	Physical content
Projects Dossier	Provides a list of projects required to deliver the Blueprint, with high-level information and estimates	The list of projects that will be required to deliver the capability defined in the Blueprint
		Outline information on outputs, timescales, resource requirements and dependencies with other projects and activities
		Dependency network
		Links showing what contribution each project and major activity will make to the programme outcomes and benefits
		Cross-reference to the Benefits Map and Benefit Profiles
Quality Management Strategy	Used to define and establish the activities for managing quality across the programme; description of the quality assurance, review and control processes for the programme covering:	What will be subject to quality assurance, review and control and the quality criteria to be applied
		A description of the functions, roles and responsibilities for quality management, aligned with the programme's organization structure
		What will trigger these activities (time-based, event-based, or associated with risk occurrence)
		What actions will be taken depending on the results of quality checks and the thresholds for escalation
		Criteria to assess programme success
		Interfaces with and dependencies on corporate management systems, including information requirements to support quality management
		Interfaces that projects will have with their programme and dependencies they will have on quality management systems set up by the programme, including information requirements to support their quality management
		Procedures for use of support tools for quality management activities, for example, change control software
		Guidelines to ensure the appropriate use of audits and health checks
		Resource requirements for quality management
		Specific standards, regulations etc. that need to be adhered to, and the subject-matter experts who will be required to support quality management with regard to these areas

Title	Purpose	Physical content
		Budgeting requirements for quality to include, but not limited to, managing contingency; accounting procedures for managing such budgets
		Cost and expenditure profile across the programme; to cover the direct cost of quality activities, and anticipated rate of usage of the contingency budget
Resource Management Strategy	Used to identify how the programme will acquire and manage the resources required to achieve the business change	Funding requirements; accounting procedures for costs and expenditure; budgets for programme management resources and funding sources
		Procurement approach and reference to current contract frameworks or arrangements that will be used
		Cost and expenditure profile across the programme, expenditure approval procedures, financial reporting procedures
		Assets required, such as buildings and office equipment to deliver the programme
		Technology and services required
		Profile of resources that are shared across more than one of the projects within the portfolio; should indicate the expected use by each project of the shared resource within time periods
		Explanation of how the manning requirements of the programme and projects will be achieved; consideration should be given to how the business operations capacity to resource the consequences of programme change will be managed
		Which subject-matter experts will be required and how they will be sourced
		Description of how the human resource requirements of the programme will be managed
		Explanation of how the mix of internal and external resources to the programme and projects will be managed
		How any necessary skills and knowledge will be transferred into business operations to establish the ongoing change
		Approach to dispute resolution where resourcing conflicts occur with business operational requirements, other initiatives and programmes

Title	Purpose	Physical content
Risk Management Strategy	Defines the programme approach to establishing its framework for risk management; content derived from the organization's risk management policy and risk management process guidance	Purpose and owner of the strategy
		Summary of the programme to which the plan relates
		Roles and responsibilities for managing risk in the programme
		The process to be used and how it has been adapted from the Risk Management Process Guide if necessary
		Any preferred techniques to be used for each step of the process described above
		Scales for estimating probability and impact, giving the criteria to be used for each level within the scale
		Guidance on calculating expected value for all the risks associated with a programme
		Guidance on how proximity for risks is to be assessed
		Risk response categories, including threats and opportunities
		Budget required to support risk management throughout the life of the programme
		Templates to be used
		Relevant early-warning indicators
		Timing of risk management activities; when formal risk management activities are to be undertaken, e.g. as part of end-of-tranche reviews
		Reports that are to be produced and their purpose, timing and recipients
		Criteria to be used to assess the effectiveness of risk management within the programmes
		The external or internal risk management standards that will be applied

Title	Purpose	Physical content
Stakeholder Engagement Strategy	Used to define the framework that will enable effective stakeholder engagement and communication	Criteria on how stakeholders with be grouped and tracked by the programme; it may be necessary to track specific key individuals and roles as well as groups
		How the analysis of a stakeholder's influence and interest in the programme will be measured and assessed
		How the importance and impact of a stakeholder to a programme will be assessed
		How stakeholder analysis information will be processed and stored
		Review cycle
		Explanation of how projects and the programme will interface on communications and stakeholder activities
		Guidelines on communications responsibilities where there is an overlap between individual project and programme roles
		Description of how the programme will engage with all stakeholders, including mechanisms for encouraging, receiving and responding to feedback from stakeholders
		Any policies on types of terminology and language that will be adopted within the programme
		Measures to determine how well the communication process is engaging with stakeholders
		Description of how the overall responsibilities for stakeholder engagement within the programme will be achieved; should include clarification of the roles of projects and business Change Teams to provide clarity and avoid overlap

Title	Purpose	Physical content
Vision Statement	Used to communicate the end goal of the programme. Could be seen as providing an external artist's impression of the desired future state	Created during 'Identifying a Programme' as part of the Programme Brief; verified and finalized during 'Defining a Programme'
		Clear statement of end goal of the programme
		Imposed constraints
		Providing context for the programme and project teams
		Any relevant information to help set expectations and context within the broader business context
		Terminology used should be suited to all stakeholders and the context of the programme

Example agendas for key programme meetings

B

Appendix B: Example agendas for key programme meetings

The following agendas are suggestions for the subjects that might be covered at key meetings during the programme. Each agenda is a roadmap for the meeting, providing a sense of purpose and direction, and making it easier to record what decisions were taken.

Each item on the agenda has been identified with the role responsible for addressing it at the meeting and the supporting roles that will be responsible for identifying and collating the information required for the item.

Each agenda has a suggested list of attendees, not all of whom will appear in the actual agenda, as not all attendees will present items from the agenda. A suggestion is made for the chairperson of the meeting, but this is only a suggestion.

BENEFIT REVIEW

Attendees

- SRO – chairperson
- Programme Manager
- Business Change Managers
- Programme Office
- Operational Managers impacted by the transition
- Project Managers of projects that have delivered outputs to the operational areas

Agenda

No.	Agenda item	Role responsible	Providers of supporting information
1	Summary of current situation: this should explain where the programme is against the Programme Plan, and provide a status report on the current tranche. This should include details of the projects that have delivered outcomes so far, and areas of the operation that are in transition	Programme Manager	Programme Office, collating progress reports from the Project Managers and the Business Change Manager(s)
2	Presentation of the relevant Benefit Profiles. This confirms to the attendees which benefits are to be reviewed and provides them with an opportunity to ask any questions about the nature of the benefit before the detailed review begins	Business Change Manager	Business Change Manager with support from the Programme Office
3	Presentation of performance information for each of the impacted operations. This information will include: ■ Original and revised performance indicators ■ Overview of the current risks facing the operation ■ Costs of transition ■ Atmosphere/level of support for changes by staff Comparison against the measures originally included in the Benefits Realization Plan will be helpful in demonstrating achievement/non-achievement	Business Change Manager	Impacted Operational Managers and Programme Office for collation of data provided by these managers
4	Summary of tangible benefits. These include measurable, financial benefits such as: ■ Reduction in processing costs ■ Reduction in headcount ■ Reduction in processing time ■ Reduction in amount of materials used per transaction ■ Increase in revenue per staff member, per customer etc. Comparison against the measures originally included in the Benefits Realization Plan will be helpful in demonstrating achievement/non-achievement	Business Change Manager	Impacted Operational Managers and Programme Office for collation of data provided by these managers

No.	Agenda item	Role responsible	Providers of supporting information
5	Summary of intangible benefits, including: ■ Perception of the organization by customers, suppliers and partner organizations ■ Media profile of the organization ■ Perception by staff of the working conditions, their position in the organization etc.	Business Change Manager	Impacted Operational Managers and Programme Office for collation of data provided by these managers
6	Identification of any risks and/or issues that directly relate to the realization of these benefits, and the responses that are in place to address them	Programme Manager	Business Change Manager
	Ensure that any required changes within the operational environment needed to respond to the risks have been made		Impacted Operational Managers
7	Summary of dis-benefits, and a review by the impacted stakeholders of their willingness to accept these dis-benefits in the longer term	Business Change Manager	Programme Office with information from impacted stakeholders
8	Identification of any unplanned benefits that have materialized as a result of transition activities	Business Change Manager	Impacted Operational Managers and Programme Office for collation of data provided by these managers
9	Identification of any unplanned dis-benefits that have materialized as a result of transition activities	Business Change Manager	Impacted Operational Managers and Programme Office for collation of data provided by these managers
10	Trend analysis: this is an explanation of the likely performance levels if the achievement of the benefits continues at current levels. It should also provide an opportunity to conclude when, if relevant, any further Benefits Reviews should be scheduled.	Business Change Manager	Impacted Operational Managers and Programme Office for collation of data provided by these managers
11	Overview of the contribution that the benefit has made at the programme level to the achievement of the programme's Business Case	Programme Manager	Programme Office

END-OF-TRANCHE REVIEW

Attendees

- Sponsoring Group
- SRO – chairperson
- Programme Manager
- Business Change Manager(s)
- Programme Office
- Operational Managers impacted by the transition
- Project Managers of projects that have delivered or will be delivering outputs to the operational areas

Agenda

These items are in addition to the items for a Benefit Review, which is likely to take place as part of an End-of-Tranche Review.

No.	Agenda item	Role responsible	Providers of supporting information
1	Confirmation that Blueprint is still aligned with corporate strategy and direction, and that the Sponsoring Group continues to support the Blueprint	SRO	Programme Manager
2	Confirmation that the Projects Dossier contains all necessary projects to deliver the Blueprint	Programme Manager	Programme Office
3	Confirmation that the programme is still justified, using the up-to-date Business Case	SRO	Programme Manager
4	Confirmation of changes to the programme team in preparation for the next tranche	Programme Manager	Programme Office
5	Confirmation that the Programme Plan reflects the Projects Dossier and related transition activities, and that there is support for this plan for the next tranche	Programme Manager	Programme Office
6	Confirmation that the governance arrangements are still appropriate and relevant and can be applied to the next tranche	Programme Manager	Programme Office

PROJECT INITIATION MEETING

Attendees

- Programme Manager – chairperson
- Programme Office
- Project Executive
- Other members of the Project Board – if they have been identified at this point
- Project Manager
- Project Assurance – if appointed

Agenda

No.	Agenda item	Role responsible	Providers of supporting information
1	Confirmation of the appointment of the Project Executive and the Project Manager	Programme Manager	
2	Presentation of the Programme Plan, including details of all projects that are due to take place in this current tranche. This is a scene-setting item, providing relevant information to the project team of the interdependencies of its outputs to other outputs that the tranche must deliver	Programme Manager	Programme Office
3	Walk-through of the Project Brief: ■ Objectives ■ Scope ■ Exclusions ■ Expected outputs It is important to carefully explain exclusions and expected outputs as these will have been decided in relation to other projects that are taking place in the tranche, and derived from the Blueprint, which might not be visible to the project team	Programme Manager	Programme Office
4	Confirmation of expected budget and schedule of delivery for the project, and any tolerances on this amount so that the project team can create the Project Plan and Project Initiation Document	Programme Office	Levels specified by the Programme Manager, but collated against all other projects by the Programme Office

No.	Agenda item	Role responsible	Providers of supporting information
5	Confirmation of the approach to risk management and change control, and agreement on the escalation route for those items that require decisions at the programme level or above	Programme Office	Escalation route designed by the Programme Office and agreed with the Programme Manager and SRO
6	Review of the quality management processes that apply to the programme and any specific quality standards that the project must adhere to	Programme Manager	Programme Office
7	Presentation of the programme Communications Plan and a discussion/agreement on the approach to stakeholder communication that will be taken by the project team	Programme Office	Communication activities are carried out by the Programme Office, in accordance with the programme-level Communications Plan created by the Programme Manager
8	Explanation of the approach to progress reporting that is being taken across the programme as a whole and an explanation of the requirement for reporting from this project specifically	Programme Office	Programme Office

POST-PROJECT REVIEW

Attendees

- Programme Manager – chairperson
- Business Change Manager
- Programme Office
- Project Executive
- Project Manager
- Project Assurance

Agenda

No.	Agenda item	Role responsible	Providers of supporting information
1	Summary of current situation. This should provide summary data about the project, including when it went live and what operational areas were immediately impacted, and identify any areas that have been impacted subsequently	Programme Manager	Programme Office, collating progress reports from the Project Managers and the Business Change Manager(s)
2	Presentation of the Business Case for the project, with up-to-date information against each of the items in the Business Case, specifically:	Project Executive	Business Change Manager and Programme Office
	■ Total costs of delivery of the outputs from the project		
	■ Previous and current performance measures for each of the benefits listed		
	■ Confirmation that all risks related to the operation have an owner and are being managed		

RISK MANAGEMENT WORKSHOP

Attendees

- Programme Manager – chairperson
- Business Change Manager
- Programme Office
- Quality Manager(s)
- Internal Auditors
- Compliance Manager(s)
- Risk Manager(s)
- Project Assurance
- Project Managers
- Operational Managers

Agenda

No.	Agenda item	Role responsible	Providers of supporting information
1	Presentation of the risk management system in use across the organization. This ensures that all members of the programme team are well informed and reduces the risk that the programme will create an approach to risk management that is out of step with the existing process	Risk Manager	Internal Audit, Compliance Manager(s)
2	Review of the sources and types of risk that will arise from: ■ Projects ■ Transition activities Use lessons learned from other projects and programmes that have taken place in the organization, and refer to experts in the related area, if necessary from consultancies or suppliers	Programme Manager	Programme Office, which may source experts to address or facilitate the workshop
3	Confirmation of the mechanism to be used for deciding on the levels of probability and impact for each risk. Explain and give examples to ensure that as much information as possible is transferred from the programme to the individual projects	Programme Manager	Programme Office
4	Confirmation of the monitoring and control framework to be in place between the projects, the operational areas where transition will take place, and the programme team	Programme Manager	Programme Office
5	Agree the format of the Risk Register and ensure there is clarity over each item on the register so that there will be uniformity in how it is used by the projects and operational areas	Programme Manager	Programme Office

QUALITY MANAGEMENT WORKSHOP

Attendees

- Programme Manager – chairperson
- Business Change Manager
- Programme Office
- Quality Manager(s)
- Internal Auditors
- Compliance Manager(s)
- Project Assurance

Agenda

No.	Agenda item	Role responsible	Providers of supporting information
1	Presentation of the quality management system in use across the organization. This ensures that all members of the programme team are well informed and reduces the risk that the programme will create an approach to quality that is out of step with the existing process	Quality Manager	Internal Audit
			Compliance Manager(s)
			Operational Managers
2	Configuration Management approach for all classes of assets including:	Programme Office	Internal Audit, other programme managers
	■ Programme documentation		
	■ Project documentation		
	■ Documentation from external suppliers and partner organizations		
	■ New software and IT systems		
	■ Other physical products		

Further information

Further information

Do you think you are ready to learn more about MSP? The links and publications listed below will give you a greater level of understanding and put you in contact with the rest of the MSP community.

PUBLICATIONS

Your first stop will be the Managing Successful Programmes manual:

Managing Successful Programmes (MSP)
ISBN 9780113310401

Business Benefits through Programme and Project Management
ISBN 9780113310258

MSP Pocketbook
ISBN 9780113310654

These publications are available in a variety of formats and can be purchased from the Best Management Practice website (www.best-management-practice.com).

USEFUL LINKS

www.best-management-practice.com

www.usergroup.org.uk (the official Best Practice user group)

OTHER RELATED PUBLICATIONS

Managing Successful Projects with PRINCE2™
ISBN 9780113309467

Management of Risk: Guidance for Practitioners
ISBN 9780113310388

ACCREDITATION

Foundation Examination

This is a short answer/multiple-choice style examination with 50 questions to be completed in 40 minutes. You need to answer 25 questions correctly to pass, i.e. gain a pass mark of 50% or above to pass. This is a closed-book examination, and to do well you will need to be familiar with the structure of programme management including having an understanding of what happens in each element of the Transformational Flow, who is responsible for and what each of the Themes contributes to the programme, and the documentation that is produced when applying these Themes.

Practitioner Examination

This is a scenario-based question paper with one programme scenario and nine sections, each worth 20 marks and covering different parts of the syllabus. All sections have up to three questions and are compulsory. You need to score 90 marks to pass. The examination lasts for 150 minutes, and there is no set reading time. Ensure that you give yourself sufficient time to become familiar with the scenario in the examination paper and to understand the format of the questions.

This is also a closed-book examination. However, the exam is not a memory test – the examiner will provide you with all the relevant information about the products that you will need. They are interested in your ability to demonstrate that you can use the MSP Transformational Flow, Themes and Control Documents to deal with the programme scenario with which you have been presented. Therefore, although your answers will be based on the manual, you will need a good level of understanding to identify the correct answers.

Advanced Practitioner Examination

This is an open-book-style written examination, which means that you can use paper-based reference materials while taking the exam, including the MSP manual and notes that you have made during your pre-course and course work. It is worth bearing this in mind as you undertake your pre-course preparation and your revision, as you can make notes and underline key phrases in the manual that may be of help to you during the examination.

The examination lasts for 150 minutes, and there is no set reading time. Ensure that you give yourself sufficient time to become familiar with the information supplied by the examiner regarding an aspect of the case study on which they would like you to concentrate. The examination is out of 75 marks and you need to get 38 marks to pass. The marks are not distributed evenly among the questions – some are worth more than others, but this will be shown on the paper.

The examination is based on the MSPCare case study and consists of up to three questions which may be subdivided. It is very much a practical application. You are being asked to apply your knowledge of programme management to the MSPCare programme, so your answers must include relevant material from the case study and should be based on your experience of working in or with programmes.

For more information on accredited training organizations for MSP and the examinations please visit the MSP website (www.programmes.org).

Glossary

Glossary

Assurance

All the systematic actions necessary to provide confidence that the target [system, process, organization, programme, project, outcome, benefit, capability, product output, deliverable] is appropriate. Appropriateness might be defined subjectively or objectively in different circumstances. The implication is that assurance will have a level of independence from that which is being assured.

Baseline

Reference levels against which an entity is monitored and controlled.

Benefit/s

The measurable improvement resulting from an outcome perceived as an advantage by one or more stakeholders.

Benefits Management

The identification, definition, tracking, realization and optimization of benefits, usually within a programme.

Benefits Realization Plan

A complete view of all the Benefit Profiles in the form of a schedule.

Best Practice

A defined and proven method of managing events effectively.

Blueprint

A model of the business or organization, its working practices and processes, the information it requires and the technology that will be needed to deliver the capability described in the Vision Statement.

Business Case

The justification for an organizational activity [strategic, programme, project, operational] which typically contains costs, benefits, risks and timescales and against which continuing viability is tested.

Business Change Manager

The role responsible for benefits management, from identification through to realization, and ensuring the implementation and embedding of the new capabilities delivered by the projects. Typically allocated to more than one individual. Alternative title: 'Change Agent'.

Capability

A service, function or operation that enables an organization to exploit opportunities

Change Manager

Reports to the Business Change Manager and may operate at a project level to support benefits realization, focusing on the realization of a particular benefit.

Change Team

A group of specialists appointed to support the Business Change Manager in the business change management aspects of benefits realization.

Configuration management

Technical and administrative activities concerned with the creation, maintenance and controlled change of configuration throughout the life of a product.

Corporate Governance

The ongoing activity of maintaining a sound system of internal control by which the directors and officers of an organization ensure that effective management systems, including financial monitoring and control systems, have been put in place to protect assets, earning capacity and the reputation of the organization.

Dis-benefit

Outcomes perceived as negative by one or more stakeholders. Dis-benefits are actual consequences of an activity whereas, by definition, a risk has some uncertainty about whether it will materialize.

Governance

The functions, responsibilities, processes and procedures that define how a programme is set up, managed and controlled.

Issue

A relevant event that has happened, was not planned and requires management action. Could be a problem, query, concern, change request or risk that has occurred.

Leadership

Leadership is the ability to direct, influence and motivate others towards a better outcome.

Opportunity

An uncertain event that could have a favourable impact on objectives or benefits.

Outcome

The result of change, normally affecting real-world behaviour and/or circumstances. Outcomes are desired when a change is conceived. Outcomes are achieved as a result of the activities undertaken to effect the change. In a programme, the outcome is the manifestation of part or all of the new state conceived in the Blueprint.

Output

The tangible or intangible product resulting from a planned activity.

Plan

A detailed proposal for doing or achieving something detailing the what, when, how and by whom.

Policy

A course of action (or principle) adopted by an organization. A business state of intent, setting the tone for an organization's culture.

Portfolio

All the programmes and stand-alone projects being undertaken by an organization, a group of organizations or an organizational unit.

Product

An input or output, whether tangible or intangible, that can be described in advance, created and tested. Also known as an output or deliverable.

Programme

Temporary flexible organization structure created to coordinate, direct and oversee the implementation of a set of related projects and activities in order to deliver outcomes and benefits related to an organization's strategic objectives. A programme is likely to have a life that spans several years.

Programme Board

A group that is established to support the SRO to deliver the programme.

Programme management

The coordinated organization, direction and implementation of a dossier of projects and transformation activities (i.e. the programme) to achieve outcomes and realize benefits of strategic importance.

Programme Manager

The role responsible for the set-up, management and delivery of the programme. Typically allocated to a single individual.

Programme Office

The function providing the information hub for the programme and its delivery objectives; would provide support for more than one programme.

Programme Organization

How a programme will be managed throughout its lifecycle, the roles and responsibilities of individuals involved in the programme, and personnel management or human resources arrangements.

Project

A temporary organization that is created for the purpose of delivering one or more business products according to a specified Business Case.

Project Brief

Statement that describes the purpose, cost, time and performance requirements/constraints for a project.

Quality

The totality of features and inherent or assigned characteristics of a product, person, process, service and/or system that bear on its ability to show that it meets expectations or stated needs, requirements or specifications.

Quality assurance

Independent check that products will be fit for purpose or meet requirements.

Quality management system

The complete set of quality standards, procedures and responsibilities for a site or an organization.

Risk

An uncertain event or set of events which, should it occur, will have an effect on the achievement of objectives. A risk is measured by a combination of the probability of a perceived threat or opportunity occurring and the magnitude of its impact on objectives.

Risk assessment

The identification and evaluation of risks.

Risk estimation

The estimation of probability and impact of an individual risk, taking into account predetermined standards, target risk levels, interdependencies and other relevant factors.

Risk management

The systematic application of principles, approach and processes to the tasks of identifying and assessing risks, and then planning and implementing risk responses.

Senior Responsible Owner

The single individual with overall responsibility for ensuring that a project or programme meets its objectives and delivers the projected benefits.

Sponsor

The main driving force behind a programme or project.

Sponsoring Group

The main driving force behind a programme that provides the investment decision and top-level endorsement of the rationale and objectives of the programme.

Stakeholder

Any individual, group or organization that can affect, be affected by, or perceive itself to be affected by, an initiative (programme, project, activity, risk).

Strategy

An approach or line to take, designed to achieve a long-term aim. Strategies can exist at different levels in an organization – in MSP there are corporate strategies for achieving objectives that will give rise to programmes. Programmes then develop strategies aligned with these corporate objectives against particular delivery areas.

Threat

An uncertain event which could have a negative impact on objectives or benefits.

Tranche

A group of projects structured around distinct step changes in capability and benefit delivery.

Transformation

A distinct change to the way an organization conducts all or part of its business.

Index

Index